WHERE THE BROOK AND RIVER MEET

Life in Lincolnshire Titles

This is the tenth in the **Life in Lincolnshire** series of titles. Further details may be found inside the back cover or on the back flap of the cased edition.

WHERE THE BROOK AND RIVER MEET

MEMORIES OF A LINCOLNSHIRE CHILDHOOD

by

SUE FLAVELL

1970  1994

RICHARD KAY
80 SLEAFORD ROAD • BOSTON • LINCOLNSHIRE • PE21 8EU

The right of Sue Flavell to be regarded as the author of this work is hereby asserted in accordance with the provisions of the Copyright, Designs, and Patents Act 1988.

The book has been typeset by the publisher using an ®AppleMac computer with ®Microsoft Word and ®PageMaker applications. The main body of the text is set in ™Bookman 10 point type.
Printed by The Echo Press • Jubilee Drive • Belton Park • Loughborough • Leicestershire LE11 0XS

FOR SOPHIE AND BENJAMIN

ACKNOWLEDGEMENTS

I am most grateful to the following for their help: Sally Blake (née Wyndham-Davies); Elsie Borman; Jill and Colin Daniels; Nan Finn; Hilary Giltrap; Carol Hammond; Maureen and Michael Joseph; David Robinson; Alison Thomas; Jenny Walton; the staffs of Nettleham Library, Lincoln Central Library, and the Music and Drama Library . . . and particularly to my mother, Joyce Eyre (who denies everything). Any errors are my own.

I am indebted to Sarah Jennings for the drawing on the cover.

The book was serialised on BBC Radio Lincolnshire from October 1993–January 1994. A very special thank you to Dave Bussey, who produced the programmes, for his help and enthusiasm.

Information about James Joyce came from *Nora, A Biography of Nora Joyce*, by Brenda Maddox, New York, Ballentine Books, 1988.

ILLUSTRATIONS

No.

page

The Author's Parents
in earlier years

ILLUSTRATION ACKNOWLEDGEMENTS

Both the author and the publisher are grateful for the help accorded in obtaining the photographs. Many are the personal property of the author, her family and friends: in some instances with no knowledge of who took the particular photograph and thus the copyright owner. We are particularly grateful for help in obtaining the following, for the loan of copies for reproduction and, for permission to reproduce the photographs: Lincolnshire Echo, 12, 15; Sheffield Telegraph, 24.

Despite extensive enquiries it has not been found possible to identify the origins of some others. If we have inadvertently infringed copyright we apologise and shall be glad to know any details. Photographs have kindly been loaned by the following and, where ownership of the copyright has been known permission to reproduce has been given. If we have failed to achieve contact we shall be glad if the copyright owner will inform the publisher.

Christ's Hospital School, Lincoln, 17, 18, 19, 20, 21, 22; Joy and Don Comber, 25a, b, c; House of Fraser, 12; Hilary Giltrap, 26; Maisie Hindle, 24; Lincolnshire County Council, Recreational Services: Local Studues Collection, Lincoln Central Library, 13, 28; Patty Phillips, 8, 11, 16; Fred Trott, 14; Pearl Vose, 2, 3; Art Walker, 29, 30, 32; Sally Wyndham-Davies, 27;

MAIDENHOOD

by

HENRY WADSWORTH LONGFELLOW

Maiden! with the meek, brown eyes
In whose orbs a shadow lies,
Like the dusk in evening skies!

Thou whose locks outshine the sun,
Golden tresses, wreathed in one,
As the braided streamlets run!

Standing, with reluctant feet,
Where the brook and river meet,
Womanhood and childhood fleet!

Gazing, with a timid glance,
On the brooklet's swift advance,
On the river's broad expanse!

Deep and still, that gliding stream
Beautiful to thee must seem,
As the river of a dream.

Then why pause with indecision,
When bright angels in thy vision
Beckon thee to fields Elysian?

Seest thou shadows sailing by,
As the dove, with startled eye,
Sees the falcon's shadow fly?

Hearest thou voices on the shore,
That our ears perceive no more,
Deafened by the cataract's roar?

O, thou child of many prayers!
Life hath quicksands,—Life hath snares!
Care and age come unawares!

Like the swell of some sweet tune,
Morning rises into noon,
May glides onward into June.

Childhood is the bough, where slumbered
Birds and blossoms many-numbered; –
Age, that bough with snows encumbered.

Gather, then, each flower that grows,
When the young heart overflows,
To embalm that tent of snows.

Bear a lily in thy hand;
Gates of brass cannot withstand
One touch of that magic wand.

Bear through sorrow, wrong, and ruth,
In thy heart the dew of youth,
On thy lips the smile of truth.

Oh, that dew, like balm, shall steal
Into wounds, that cannot heal,
Even as sleep our eyes doth seal;

And that smile, like sunshine, dart
Into many a sunless heart,
For a smile of God thou art.

With Mother and sister Jill — 1948

1.

WE MOVED TO NETTLEHAM in January 1945 on a bitterly cold night during the blackout. No welcoming lights shone from windows and our arrival, in a removal van, was made even gloomier by a fierce snowstorm. Or so I am told. I was a year old and, at that time, my parents' only child.

A family of urban Yorkshire Puddings who had survived the blitz in Sheffield – my father was a metallurgist who had spent the war testing steel for aircraft and armaments – we entered a close-knit rural community of Yellow Bellies. Many of them were descendants of old Nettleham families: Kettle, Dawson, Straw, Clipsham, Warwick, mentioned in the parish records over two hundred years earlier.

Some of the residents could have been lifted from a pack of *Happy Families* playing cards: Sooty Yarnell the Sweep; Mr. Postman Richardson; Mrs. Laundry Richardson; Charlie Trott and his buses; Nurse Heath the district nurse and midwife; Granny Sawyer and her twenty-one children; Mr. Scarborough the rosy-cheeked butcher; and the aptly-named Larder brothers who kept the provisions store on the village green.

The heart of Nettleham was a cluster of properties around the village green, one of which my parents rented for five shillings a week. It lacked electricity and was lit by gas. Accustomed to a city's modern plumbing, they were shocked to discover that they were expected to share an outside closet with the family next door (my father speedily provided our own). They were even more shocked when they saw Matt and his horse-drawn dilly cart stop on the green once a week to empty the buckets – Matt carrying them across on his shoulder. There is a story, one hopes apocryphal, that the bottom once fell out of a full bucket before Matt reached the cart.

When the war ended in September 1945, I was too young to hear the collective sigh of relief when sons, fiancés and husbands returned safely to the village, I was also too young to sense the communal sadness that eight names would shortly be added to the First World War memorial on Nettleham Green.

However difficult it was post-war, with rationing lasting longer than anyone expected, and the looming spectre of the Cold War, nevertheless the late forties were the beginning of a kind of subdued golden age. However spartan life might be, it was good to be alive. Society was family oriented; people counted their blessings and looked after one another. They showed contempt for the spivs – the black marketeers and profiteers who were eager to gain from the shortages.

There was a fierce pride in being British: we'd won the war. In Lincolnshire, with its many aerodromes, the population had lived with the constant thrumming of bombers on their way to Germany and drunk in the local pubs with the young RAF pilots and crews; many of whom were there one evening and gone for ever the next – a tragic, daily reminder of the courageous part they had played in our victory. Nettleham also had a close personal link with the Dam Buster squadron, a few miles away at Scampton, for Guy Gibson's batman, Crosby, understandably nicknamed 'Bing', lived in the village.

In many respects it was easier to pick up the pieces in a rural community. Those who had survived the war in the cities, witnessing appalling destruction and loss of life, had to rebuild both their homes and their lives. In the country, the remorseless and demanding rhythm of the seasons and work on the land had provided a deep sense of continuity which, whatever the disruptions, had remained intact. By a cruel irony, it was the weather immediately after the war which violently disrupted the farmer's efforts to increase food production and to reclaim some of the many acres of land which had been taken over by the War Office for additional aerodromes in Lincolnshire. The winter of 1946-47 brought the most serious blizzards and the greatest freeze-up for over a century. On Greetwell Lane, leading from Wragby Road to Nettleham, the snow froze to the height of the tops of the hedgerows. Some of the worst recorded floods in Britain followed the Big Thaw in March.

My first clear memory was the excitement, some months later, when the then Princess Elizabeth married Prince Philip in November 1947; a fairy-tale romance of a beautiful young princess and handsome foreign prince which provided a timely and glittering antidote to the post-war austerity. I spent many happy and messy hours wielding a blunt pair of scissors, untidily cutting out newspaper and magazine photographs of the wedding and sticking them with the aid of lumpy flour paste into a thick brown scrapbook.

At the age of four, I learned to read by picking out newspaper headlines while curled contentedly on my father's lap. My subsequent descriptions of childhood adventures were quaint reminders of the dramas in Berlin and ministerial missions which I had unwittingly absorbed. I'd return home after a squabble with my friends and explain there had been something of a crisis and an agreement had not been reached.

For my sixth birthday, my Great Aunt Carrie gave me a copy of *The Pilgrim's Progress* by John Bunyan. I can still remember that reading it was a hard slog but the terrible description of the Slough of Despond stuck forcibly in my mind and whenever I thought of Matt stooping under the weight of a full dilly bucket I couldn't help but think of poor Christian. Many years later I learned that in May 1811, Robert Bunyan, the last male descendant of author John, had been fined thirteen shillings and fourpence for non-attendance at Nettleham Court. In those days, all residents and tenants in the village had, by law, to attend any proceedings.

Those achingly idyllic English country gardens – a rhapsody of lupins, hollyhocks, night-scented stocks and red roses around the door – which were depicted so colourfully on my jigsaw puzzles, were far from the rural reality after the war. Gardens were there to provide food and Nettleham was remarkably self-sufficient.

Our own garden was a pathetic sight. My parents, urban to the core, were sadly lacking in green fingers. If they'd had to dig for victory the war would have been lost. At the harvest festival when Nettleham church was aglow with giant fruit and vegetables

– onions the size of footballs glowing with a silken sheen, crisp, burnished apples, a veritable still life of the fruits of field and garden – we felt even more like outsiders. Unable to contribute anything other than praise, we stood in impotent admiration before the villagers' efforts.

We kept a few chickens, but only for eggs. With the townie's sentimental attachment to animals as pets, however much we enjoyed meat (rationed until 1956), killing them for the pot was traumatic. When my father once brought himself to do the deed, he closed his eyes and, grimacing painfully, wrung the chicken's neck. When it squawked in indignation my father dropped it. The chicken furiously re-arranged its neck and scampered off. All our chickens died of old age.

Sybil and Walter Bratley, our neighbours, had three sons: Derek, Alan and Colin, some years my senior. The boys treated me with great patience and gentleness and as far as I was concerned they could do no wrong. Neither could their father; for Mr. Bratley made ice-cream in the shed behind the cottage. It was sold only on Sunday afternoons when there would be a queue of Nettleham residents in the garden, lining up eagerly for a weekly treat. For a small girl to live in such close proximity to ice-cream was the nearest thing to Heaven.

My mother, when speaking of my father to friends. always used his Christian name. Mrs. Bratley frequently referred to Mr. Bratley as 'Dad'. I suppose it was understandable that, as a toddler, I assumed that this must be his Christian name. One evening returning to Nettleham on Mr. Trott's full workman's bus and sitting on my mother's lap, I spotted Mr. Bratley getting on. 'Look Mummy,' I yelled delightedly to a crowded bus: 'There's Dad!'

Larder's shop on the village green, with its canisters of flour and sugar, medicinal compounds and freshly baked bread was a wonderland to a child; a sensual experience. In our present pursuit of hygiene, we have forgotten how good smells wet the appetite; that watching dried fruit and other provisions poured onto scales, being weighed and skillfully packed, is visually pleasing. In 1947, however, when food was rationed, mothers were

2. *Larder's shop on the village green*

3. *Larder's van*

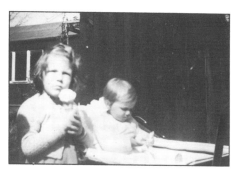

4. *Mr. Bratley's ice cream*

5.

understandably more concerned as they watched food being weighed, that there would be sufficient to feed the family.

Basic foodstuffs and clothing were on coupons; tinned foods and dried fruit, as well as chocolates and sweets, on 'points'. Rations fluctuated but an average weekly allowance per person was: 5oz of meat, $1^1/_2$ oz of cheese, 6 oz butter or marge, 1 oz cooking fat, 8 oz sugar, 2 pints milk, and one egg. Between July 1946 and July 1948 even bread was rationed.

Larder's had a separate drapery department which for many years was run by Miss Elsie Borman, one of the sweetest people in the village and still an intrinsic part of it. It smelt of clean, starched linen and was fitted with deep honey-coloured wooden shelves and silently sliding drawers filled with sheets, pillowcases, lengths of fabric and haberdashery, reels of cottons and tapes, and party ribbons for pigtails.

My sister, Jill, was born in 1948, the same year as Prince Charles. As the birth of the prince gave me the opportunity to add lots of photographic cuttings to my Royal scrapbook, I considered his arrival much more interesting than that of my sister. I can remember Dr. Lechler saying to my father shortly after my sister's birth: 'It's another girl, I'm afraid,' – a remark which would not be tolerated in these days of political correctness – and my father replying, delightedly, that that was exactly what he wanted.

At the time I wasn't sure it was exactly what *I* wanted, having been the centre of my parents' attention for almost five years. No doubt feelings of resentment and jealousy led me one morning to sulk at the bottom of the garden. No doubt it was a form of unconscious protest, rather than a conscious need to keep warm, that led me to light a forbidden match.

When the firefighters had departed and the village almost returned to normal after the excitement, I toddled around the blackened remnants of the hedge to offer my apologies to Mrs. Porter Senior for robbing her of the only barrier between her well-tended garden and our wilderness.

It was her grandson, David, who later was my little sister's best friend, or 'fwend' as David lisped. David's father, Ambrose Porter, a delightfully inventive character whose patience and eccentricities endeared him to Nettleham children, kept the local garage. He gave David a miniature prototype from R. M. Wright in Lincoln of the new post-war Austin A 40.

'Id Dilly coming?' David would ask as he drew up solemnly outside the cottage in his little pedal car to take Jill for a drive. One sunlit morning, he crossed the village green pedalling furiously and became aware of the towering bulk of Charlie Trott's bus following slowly and patiently behind like a benevolent monster breathing down the neck of Noddy. David, undaunted, continued to pedal with great aplomb until, on the far side of the green, beside the old stables and the doctor's creeper-clad house, his pudgy little hand shot out, signalling a right turn, and the car moved from beneath the bus's front bumper.

Ambrose Porter put a tiny engine into the pedal car so that David and Jill could roar up and down the drive. He removed the lavatory from an old outhouse closet, painted the walls white and offered it to us for our Secret—obviously not so secret—Society meetings. He nailed a nameplate to the door on which he had painted two words which he assured us solemnly were French: *La Vatory*.

Many years later Ambrose bought the huge organ from the Savoy cinema (now a bingo hall) in Lincoln and installed it in his barn beside Nettleham Garage. A manual, six rank Compton with melaton, considered to be one of the world's most remarkable cinema organs, it now found itself competing with the church bells as Ambrose played it in the evenings; the noise sounding like a mournful herd of cows in stereophonic lament. It finally found a home in a private cinema in Newark.

For a short time I saw the organ *in situ* at the Savoy when it rose before my eyes in a wash of gaudy rainbow colours at ABC Minors – those magical Saturday morning sessions; sixpence worth of heaven.

Bodies hurtled down aisles; kids choked on sherbert and liquorice sticks as they tried to suck and yell at the same time; school caps were thrown excitedly into the air as the Lone Ranger and faithful Tonto crested the hill just as the Injuns surrounded the wagon train; embarrassed whistles greeted the sloppy kissing close-ups; and there was the delicious danger of being sitting targets in the stalls for the little sadists in the balcony who would bite off the tip of their cornet and blow what was left of their ice-cream onto our heads below. The more timid of us shivered with delighted relief when the manager, finally losing patience, ejected the bloody-kneed Stamp End Gang – Just William every one of them – with an average age of eight. My mother soon decided it was unsuitable.

2.

I T WAS A VERY HAPPY VILLAGE CHILDHOOD. We were far from wealthy but were not, to my knowledge, ever short of money; and it was not a subject for conversation, except when a Nettleham couple won £6,000 on the football pools – a fortune in those days. This understandably provoked not only my family but the entire village into fantasising about what they would have done with such a windfall. The lucky winners bought a foreign car with some of the money – which we considered suitably exotic.

I attended Nettleham Church of England Infants and Junior School opposite the church, from the age of five. The school, a cluster of single-storey stone buildings beside a playground, was warm and cosy in the winter thanks to a pot-bellied stove.

Group photographs in the playground show little girls with be-ribboned bunches or pigtails; little boys with short trousers, knobbly knees, hand-knitted pullovers and long woollen socks.

Miss Bowins, my first teacher, and Mr. Thursby, the headmaster, were caring and patient. I loved reading and writing. I was sorry I lived only two minutes walk from school and so didn't qualify for school lunches; Mrs. Rose Hill, who prepared the meals, was a wonderful, homely cook.

During school break, the playground rang with the cheerful sounds of little boys pretending to be aeroplanes and little girls chanting the traditional rhymes as they moved through the steps of childhood games: *Ring-a-Ring-a-Roses; What Time is it Mr. Wolf?; Here We Go Round the Mulberry Bush;* and *Oranges and Lemons.* Some of this golden treasury must have been taught and yet most of it seems to have been acquired by a process of osmosis; of dipping into a community chest of folk lore accessible to successive generations but which, sadly, seems to be lost to many of today's children.

We grew mustard and cress on blotting paper; constructed and painted our Nativity scenes in a state of high anticipatory excitement at Christmas and carefully learned our three 'Rs'. In geography lessons our minds were opened to the world outside – a large part of which was still coloured a bright pink for the British Empire. We also learned about our home county of Lincolnshire. I remember writing to a canning factory in Boston and being rewarded one morning by a large envelope delivered by the postman. It contained a thick wad of pristine and brightly coloured labels for tins of fruit and vegetables: peas, carrots, peaches, plums. I was somewhat at a loss to know what to do with these once I had gloated over them, but I finally settled on sticking them into my 'Royal' scrapbook.

The dolls prams came and went. I used mine as a battering ram to get my own back on Bernard Ranshaw. In total innocence, but carelessly in my estimation, he'd run over me with his bicycle after I'd rushed headlong out of a blind alley by the fish and chip shop, tripped and fallen under his wheels. I was much prouder of the dent in the pram than of its contents which, thanks to my far from maternal efforts, looked like desperate terminal cases in a dolls' hospital.

I preferred my books: *Alice in Wonderland*, *Little Women*, Hans Anderson's often gruesome *Fairy Tales*, and my cardboard model Post Office with its dinky miniature postal orders and messy rubber stamp. I was also determined, away from my mother's watchful eye, to persuade more friends to write in my autograph album. This activity had come to a grinding halt one day and resulted in a page being torn out when mother had read a recent entry by an adult who should have known better: 'I've seen albums blue, I've seen albums red; but in Africa, where I've never been, all bums are black'.

Each summer there was the eagerly awaited Nettleham garden fête: bran tub, coconut shy, one-legged race, egg and spoon race, and fancy dress parade. I have a photograph of myself as Farmer Giles: white smock and red kerchief, and a battered trilby hat, pushing a miniature metal wheelbarrow filled with root vegetables and with a milk can dangling from my wrist. I won first prize; but my mutton chop whiskers, made from the lining of an old furry slipper and glued on, made me cry when they were yanked off after

10.

5. *Nettleham Church of England school group, 1950*

6. *Cocker in our garden*

7. *'Farmer Giles' at the garden fête*

8. *Nettleham village beck with the bank being scythed.*

my victorious appearance.

When Bill Bailey's Memorial Playing Fields opened I rubbed candle grease on the chute and slid down again and again until the shine blinded me and the chute was so slippery that I'd catapult off the end wide-eyed with shock. I went home with my knickers stiff with tallow, bow-legged like a jockey.

How did mothers keep up with the washing in those days? Machines were virtually unknown. There were no blue jeans, few man-made fibres, no biological powders. Soap was rationed until 1950. White ankle socks were scuffed within minutes. Laundry was laboriously washed with the aid of a washboard and dolly tub, mangle and Reckitt's Blue; and for many years there was no inside running water. Buckets had to be filled from the village pump near our neighbour's house. One morning the water came out a lurid shade of green. It transpired that someone from RAF Scampton had dumped chemicals into the tip at the corner of Deepdale Lane and Welton Road, The chemicals had seeped through the ground and polluted the entire village's water supply.

The village tip, (now the site of the Police Headquarters), was a desolate No-Man's Land of decaying and burning rubbish; a dangerous No-Go area for children. It was guarded by Mr. Whitby and his eager terrier which lived in a state of perpetual excitement killing the numerous rats which were drawn to such rich pickings.

Gypsies knocked regularly at our door selling pegs and lucky heather. My mother, wary of the gypsies' exoticism and ancient knowing looks, feared primitive retribution if she refused them. As a result we soon acquired enough pegs for a Chinese laundry. It's strange to think that British pop music began in the fifties when skiffle groups, like Lonnie Donnegan's, used their mother's washboard as backing for their songs.

When eventually we acquired a washing machine it cost £5 and must have been an early unsuccessful prototype. It vibrated furiously and when it reached spin dry would throw itself into a complete frenzy. My mother would call for my sister and me to leap on top of it. We'd hang on grimly, our teeth chattering from the vibration, in an attempt to stop it juddering its way across the kitchen.

We played somersaults and leapfrog, marbles and five-stones. We returned home with bruised fingers from our hardened, vinegar-soaked-conker games; the conkers collected from beneath the huge chestnut tree in the churchyard. We played French cricket, jumped cracks in paving stones for fear of descending into hell, and skipped until we were breathless; the streets blissfully free of cars, the entire village our playground. The pavements were permanently marked by the chalked runic rectangles of our hopscotch games. The word 'hopscotch', more than any other, acts as the key to unlocking my memories of childhood.

I split my leg on a rusty hinge in Valerie East's garden and was rushed across the village green by my mother to Dr. Lechler's cool, dark, tiled surgery with its intimidating antiseptic smell. Three stitches were inserted of which I was immensely proud once the initial terror had passed.

People seemed hardier in those days and would have been scornful of today's pill-popping. I remember my mother returning home after a visit to the doctor carrying a large bottle of tonic – the cure for all ills. It was black, iron-filled and evil-smelling medicine, with a metallic taste. My mother took one spoonful, grimaced with distaste, and then poured the rest down the kitchen sink. The visit alone had provided the necessary reassurance. It also provided an unwitting example to her children for we grew up with a healthy suspicion of pills and potions.

No-one dared to whinge in the presence of Nurse Heath, Nettleham's district nurse and midwife. Heathie, as she allowed her friends to call her, was a wirey, immensely strong character with a withering tongue and a scornful contempt for the self-indulgent. She had a very simple but effective way of deflating any male pomposity in later years: 'Just remember I delivered you and was the first to spank your bottom.'

A dog lover – 'They're far less trouble than humans' – she was rarely seen without a much-loved mournful-eyed whippet. Heathie's gruff exterior hid a love of humanity and much independent pride. Between her and my father was a strong mutual respect and, periodically, swallowing that pride, she would come to him for practical advice or help.

She was a tireless and devoted worker not only for the health of the residents but also for conservation long before it became a fashionable concern; so much so that the Lincolnshire Trust for Nature Conservation named one of its best nature reserves: *Heath Meadows*. Towards the end of her life, my parents took her one afternoon to visit the meadow. Losing sight of her, they found her curled up, serenely sound asleep, among the flowers. She was in her nineties when she died.

On summer afternoons after school I spent hours with my playmates lying flat on the ground, collecting grass stains on my cotton dress, searching for fairy-rings and four-leafed clovers on Back Lane. Such were the contented boundaries of our existence, and lack of media-hyped materialistic longings, that we would have found it hard to imagine what such good fortune would provide other than, perhaps, an extra ration of dolly mixtures or a taffeta party dress. Sweet rationing didn't end until 1953, and food rationing the following year. Shopping with mother always involved an element of uncertainty wondering whether there'd be sufficient coupons in the ration book.

In the evenings parents listened to the measured tones of the BBC newsreader. As children, we were unaware of the problems after the war; British Troops in Korea in 1950; the uneasy international peace, and the fears about The Bomb and the Cold War.

The wireless, to us, meant Radio Luxembourg – when we were allowed to listen to it. On evenings spent with my friend Barbara Lee, we ate our chocolate spread sandwiches and twiddled the wirelesss dial in a fervent attempt to tune in. Through the howling and tweeting we strained to hear the opening bars of the song heralding our favourite programme: 'We are the Ovalteenies, little girls and boys . . .'

A jar full of frog-spawn, collected in the village park, metamorphosed into newts and, one morning, into tiny frogs. Hopping up and down my arm, they provided a practical biology lesson. We fished in the village beck for tiddlers. You weren't considered a true Nettleham-ite until you'd fallen into the beck. Jill fell in so many times she qualified as not only a Nettleham-ite but a Kingsley Water Baby Class One. She didn't look normal without a coating of mud and slimy moss.

The beck, which meandered through the village, was Nettleham's signature. From Nettleham Road it wove its way through the meadows to Back Lane, spilling out into a pool before the old Mill House before continuing along Beckside to Vicarage Lane. Fast flowing enough to remain clean and clear. but shallow enough to allow safe paddling, it held a magnetic fascination for the village children and provided hours of healthy outdoor exercise and observation.

We would lie flat` on our tummies on one of the ricketty wooden bridges endlessly and patiently scanning the water for tiddlers, our nets and jam jars beside us at the ready. A companionable group activity, it also provided hours of concentrated and contented exploration alone if playmates weren't around; although often they were hidden round a bend intent on their own favourite patch where the moss grew thick and the pickings were rich in the shallows. One afternoon, when a child caught an eel, awesomely large by comparison with our normal catch of tiddlers and sticklebacks, children converged from all directions, tripping over their nets in their eagerness, as soon as the gleeful shout went up.

When our faces became too suffused with blood from hanging head down over the water looking for darting shadows, we'd turn somersaults on the rail of the bridge, our skirts tucked into our knickers until, finally overcome with giddiness, we'd collapse onto the bridge and dangle our legs over the side. It seems strange today, when so much money is spent on trying to keep children entertained, that it never occurred to us not to entertain ourselves. There was always too much to do and too little time before the heart sank at the sound of mother calling us home with our least favourite words: 'It's bedtime'.

Our much loved black cocker spaniel followed us everywhere, smelling very ripe. Racing to catch up with us one day as we crossed the bridge over the beck, he caught himself in the back wheels of Jill's tricycle and pitched her, the bike and himself into the water. Cocker, as we called him, without a trace of originality, was a dashing romantic figure of a dog to us. He developed canker in his ear. On Nurse Heath's insistence – and one tended to obey when Heathie insisted – he was sent alone to consult the vet who, in her opinion, was the best in the country: the one who looked after the pets and livestock of the Princess Royal at Harewood House.

We managed to create a full scale drama out of seeing him off at Lincoln railway station where, muzzled, he was entrusted, somewhat unwillingly on our part, to the guard. We were assured by our parents that Cocker would be met on arrival in Leeds and would not have to find his way to Harewood House forlornly on foot. Reassured, we were secretly terribly impressed that, indirectly, he'd be hob-nobbing with Royalty.

The year after Cocker recovered from his ear infection he was knocked down by a Roadcar bus. My father was the one who had to go out to shovel up the remains. On returning to the house and finding his family crying fit to burst, he yelled: 'That's the last time we have an infernal animal'; and then wept himself.

My sister and I formed a secret Bible Society and solemnly read SPCK texts to one another. My mother was a committed churchgoer; my father not. It was agreed that, in fairness to them both, my sister and I should attend the Church Sunday School until we reached the age of ten at which time we should be allowed to decide for ourselves whether we wished to continue church attendance.

When I reached ten I stopped going to Sunday School. My sister Jill, however, eventually went into what my father called her 'God bothering stage' and religiously attended both the Church Sunday School and the Methodists' Sunshine Corner which was held each week in the hut at the bottom of Chapel Lane. Jill found the atmosphere of the Methodist chapel, with its uninhibited singing and evangelical openness, much more to her liking than the church's solemn Holy-God-in-His-dusty-and-dry-infinite-mercy. At chapel everything was personalised. One of the female preachers, when leading prayers, added a fervent plea one evening for her boyfriend: 'And let us pray for Eddie who's on nights this week.'

16.

3.

I N THE ABSENCE OF TELEVISION, social life revolved around community activities in the mock-timbered village institute: billiards upstairs in the male preserve; concerts, whist drives and beetle drives downstairs. There were occasional film shows – usually about leper colonies shown with the aid of an unreliable projector by visiting missionaries. These provoked mixed emotions in the village children: a desire to donate our pocket money to help those poor Africans with truncated limbs and a realisation that by doing so we'd have to forego a quarter of jelly-babies that week.

The Nettleham Girls' Friendly Society claimed us as members and here dancing was the order of the evening. These festivities, held in the village institute, were presided over by two kindly and motherly ladies, Mrs. Cotten and Mrs. Whitby.

We shuffled around the room to the scratched hiccoughing strains of a waltz played on an old wind-up gramophone, our faces buried below Mrs. Whitby's or Mrs. Cotten's generous bosom, trying not to run fingers up and down or bump our noses against the prominent vertical ridges of their corsets.

When I felt I had outgrown the society, I left without a qualm but Jill, not having given notice of her treacherous intention, was consumed by guilt and became pathologically convinced that Mrs. Whitby and Mrs. Cotten were permanently on the look-out for her. She would go to great lengths to avoid meeting them. Mrs. Whitby and Mrs. Cotten were noticeable in that they always wore hats both indoors and outdoors and, like Tweedledum and Tweedledee, were invariably together. Jill would often spot their hats at some distance away and was usually able to avoid them by diving headlong into Mr. Long's sweet shop or some other handy sanctuary until the innocent pair had sailed past.

We were frequent visitors to the Radion cinema on Newport, now the studios of BBC Radio Lincolnshire, which had re-opened in 1947. With its wide, comfortable seats and warm atmosphere it attracted family audiences. The first film I remember seeing was *The Mudlark* starring a very young Andrew Ray as a poor boy reduced to combing the dirty banks of the River Thames for anything remotely scavengeable that the tide had washed up. I don't recall whether or not it had a happy ending – it probably did in those days – but I do recall feeling grateful that after the film I would be returning to my secure and cosy home.

My paternal grandparents took us each year to the pantomime at the Theatre Royal in Lincoln. Jill and I wore our matching grey flannel coats, long grey socks and red ribbons in our hair.

During one pantomime when Sandy Daw asked for volunteers to join him in the traditional childrens' sing-a-long, when the lyrics descend from the flies on a large sheet of canvas, I slid low in my seat too timid to consider such an invitation and fearful that someone might try to persuade me. My sister, however, calmly rose from her seat and edged her away along the row to the aisle.

When the song was over and the other children had returned to the auditorium Jill decided to stay where she was, staring serenely ahead, perfectly composed. This was a gift to any comedian and Sandy Daw made the most of it. He and Jill sang a duet together: 'There's a worm at the bottom of the garden, and its name is Wiggerly Woo.' At the end of the song Sandy Daw solemnly thanked Jill and gave her sixpence. Jill, equally solemnly, thanked him for the sixpence and refused to budge. He gave her another sixpence. She nodded her thanks and calmly continued to stand beside him. Whether Sandy Daw finally ran out of money or Jill decided with some innate dramatic instinct that the scene should not be milked, she finally left the stage to delighted applause when her pay-out had reached half-a-crown.

Unlike today, children's presents then were largely confined to Christmas and birthdays, with chocolate bunnies and eggs at Easter. My birthday parties were held in the village institute; trestle tables spread with Lincolnshire potted meat sandwiches, jelly, lurid blancmanges, and butterfly cakes. We played 'Musical Chairs', 'Pass the Parcel', 'Statues', and 'Blind Man's Buff'. As most of the village children were invited there was usually a very gratifying pile of presents for me to carry home although I had little time to enjoy them.

My mother allowed me to choose three gifts only. The others were parcelled up and sent, with a generosity definitely more my mother's than my own, to the Childrens' Home on St. Giles in Lincoln. In those days, pontefract cakes were a popular gift. As they tasted somewhat similar to the doctor's iron-clad medicine, I was quite happy to pass them on. But today, selfishly I admit, I regret the loss of all my childhood books and toys.

When not giving away my presents, my mother was frequently to be found at the village whist drives. She was an enthusiastic card player who hated to lose and enjoyed conducting lengthy post-mortems when she did.

During the war, when she was expecting me, she spent many nights during air-raids playing Solo with my father, her father and stepmother. The men placed bets that I would be born with a fist full of cards screaming: 'I'll go Royal Abundance!' while my mother yelled back: 'Oh no you won't. Not with *my* hand against you!'

Each summer, seven busloads of Nettleham mothers carrying rugs and baskets stuffed with sandwiches, and children clanking with buckets and spades, headed for Skegness on the annual Sunday School Outing. While my sister and I were happily occupied with playing on the sands my mother would shamelessly settle down with other mothers and play whist.

In February 1952, just after we moved from the cottage on the village green to a house in the High Street, there was a special winter treat; a bus trip to the pantomime matinee at Nottingham's Theatre Royal.

Unbeknownst to us children, King George VI had died at Sandringham. At the time the silent crowds were gathering outside the gates of Buckingham Palace, we were arriving eagerly at the theatre in Nottingham. The theatre, we soon discovered, had been closed as a mark of mourning and respect. There would be no pantomime that afternoon: no Principal Boy; no Widow Twanky.

Too young to appreciate the loss of the country's much loved king and the import of the ascension to the throne of a second Elizabeth, we were tearfully inconsolable at missing the panto and spent a miserable afternoon in an atmosphere of oppressive gloom waiting for the bus to take us back to Nettleham.

By the end of the fifties, when cars were commonplace in the village, the seven busloads to the seaside had been reduced to two. But we were one of the fortunate families who had always had a car, however decrepit, and so our treats during the intervening years had been more frequent. We caravanned at Ingoldmells long before the devastating floods, in the days when the sandhills were like mountains, thickly coated with buckthorn and seagrass; and the trippers hadn't found the spot on the map. We were miles from the crowd, snug and cosy each weekend; the caravan parked on a farm tucked in behind the sandhills at the bottom of Trunch Lane. The meadow was luxuriantly cow-splattered and yellow with kingcups which reflected butter when held beneath our chins.

'Do not touch the *deadly* nightshade!' mother would yell, managing to convey, in a way only she could, that to do so would be even more deadly than fatal. We scampered off eagerly before breakfast through a maze of berry bushes to clamber to the top of the sandhills and peer over at the sea drowning the breakwaters. We slid down on our bottoms, played hide and seek in the long grass and tramped the deserted beach.

In the crisp early morning, the smell of bacon frying would drift gradually upwards. Sniffing the air like Bisto Kids, we slipped and slithered back down the sandhills, ankles soaked with dew, returning with captured starfish and crabs in buckets and healthy appetites; not forgetting to empty our Clarke's sandals of sand before entering the caravan.

If the weather was fine, Jill and I spent the entire day with our buckets and spades determined to dig to Australia, bury father up to his neck or to stick our collection of flags onto the turrets of our slowly collapsing sandcastles. Whenever we encountered a patch of slimy mud, we remembered our mother's over-dramatic warnings about quicksands and skittered off before our bodies were sucked down with what we imagined would be deep, slurping

9. *At Skegness with Mother*

10. *Skegness – Sunday School outing*

11.
*Nettleham
Red Cross
cadets*

21.

noises of satisfaction from the sinisterly enveloping mud.

Mother swam like a porpoise in what I remember mostly as an unbroken swell of ominously cold waves. Swimming, for me, was an endurance test, not long to be endured. On with the costume, sheltering behind the breakwater, then the mad dash into the sea and the shock of the cold. Mother would still be gleefully bobbing about in the water as I splashed my frantic way out again, chiding me for my lack of enthusiasm. I dashed back up the beach, teeth chattering, stubbing toes on pebbles, to be enfolded by a towel held in the welcoming outstretched arms of my father.

There were side-trips to Skegness and Cleethorpes, the Sodom and Gomorrah of the Lincolnshire coast after the empty tranquility of Ingoldmells. We played the fruit machines with our hoarded pennies and walked the pier, feeling insecure. Looking down through the wooden boards at the dark, sinister water slapping and sucking against slimy, moss-covered pillars, we shivered at the thought of falling into Neptune's Cave. We sat entranced before Punch and Judy shows and took rides on the gentle, long-suffering donkeys; rides which lasted far too short a time. One weekend, wanting to surprise my family with a treat, I walked up the beach to secretly buy candyfloss. Returning eager to share my gifts, I raced down the beach forgetting, in the bracing wind, the delicacy of the confection. I handed over three mournfully bare sticks with a few bits of solidified sugar clinging to them.

At night we were tucked up cosily in our bunks falling asleep breathing the unmistakeable and comforting smell of calor gas. Returning from the coast on a Sunday evening we sang ourselves home: 'Tea for Two', 'You Always Hurt the One You Love', 'You Made Me Love You . . . I didn't want to do it, I didn't want to DO IT!' we would screech, almost but not quite in unison. I don't know how my father managed to concentrate through the din and avoid tipping us all into one of the many dangerous ditches on either side of the tortuous lanes which led from Ingoldmells to the main road.

Considering the noisy crowd with whom he had to share his car, it's surprising that my father's greatest relaxation was driving and we travelled many miles – summers to the caravan, autumn and winter into the countryside, – in a variety of weird and wonderful old bangers. *The Rocket*, a sarcastically named Ford, ran on a wing and a prayer. It had been purchased from a vicar in a neighbouring village. The vicar assured my father that there was no need to go for a test drive – the car was in perfect condition – and anyway, he was in a hurry to finish preparing a sermon. My father, being a trusting soul, paid his money and drove off. Shortly afterwards the car stopped. Nothing short of a miracle would make it go for any length of time. The vicar, even with his supposed hot-line to God, had clearly known his limitations.

Trips in *The Rocket* were always unpredictable. We never could be sure once we'd arrived at our destination – if we arrived – whether or not we'd be able to get home. This was no doubt one of the reasons why my mother packed enough provisions to feed a field army. Often we stopped somewhere *en route* while my father tinkered mysteriously beneath the bonnet or waited patiently, after steam had shot out of the radiator, for the engine to cool down.

My father was a natural, instinctive driver who in over forty years of motoring never so much as scratched a fender. He also possessed an unerring and infuriating instinct for travelling in the wrong direction.

While female groans and scathing remarks: 'Oh Lord, not again!' 'How does he do it?' 'Can't he read signposts like normal people?' and fingers rammed between his shoulder blades signalled him to stop, he would blithely continue driving in the direction in which he was going.

One weekend, returning in the early hours of the morning from a trip to Blackpool to see the illuminations, my sister and I, fast asleep in the back, were awoken by my mother's shrieks of laughter. Struggling up from beneath our travelling rug we saw, to our delighted astonishment, that we were driving in a slow and stately fashion down the main platform of Manchester railway station. A large, steaming locomotive was inches from the car window. A guard was chucking in mailbags. Other railway staff were regarding our car with understandable surprise. Coming through the city during the night, with his three nagging navigators briefly silent, father had inadvertently driven down the entrance to the station used by Her Majesty's mail vans.

Aunt Maud, Uncle John, and their son, Richard, who was my age, were frequent companions on our cultural excursions, although trips were never without happy incident if Aunt Maud was in the party. One Sunday we returned from Somersby after a visit to Tennyson's home reciting – most appropriately we thought – 'Come into the garden, Maud, For the black bat night has flown.' Our latest car, *Puffing Billy*, an ancient Singer overloaded with four adults and three children, refused to continue up one of the few steep hills in Lincolnshire. Aunt Maud, with a strong instinct for self-preservation, cried 'Flaming Hell!' and, leaping out at surprising speed, headed for the hedge to watch what she thought would be our untimely demise. This did not please my mother, who felt that if we were going to go we should all go together. It was disloyal of Aunt Maud to try to save herself – and very short-sighted. Imagine how lonely she would have been without the rest of the family. The truth was that mother did not relish the thought of any of us being alive to have fun if she couldn't be there to share it.

4.

THE CORONATION, IN JUNE 1953, with its magnificent pageantry, provided a joyful release from the austerity of rationing and the post-war years. It inspired a heart-warming display of patriotic loyalty and rejoicing, and the hope of a new Elizabethan Golden Age. The conquest of Everest, in May, by Edmund Hillary and Sherpa Tenzing had provided Britain with a proud curtain-raiser.

But in Lincolnshire the events at the end of January of that year tempered the mood of celebration. The devastation left after the East Coast floods, in which 300 died and over 40,000 homes were destroyed, demonstrated, tragically, that even in Britain the elements could be callously destructive on a massive scale.

We visited the coast a couple of months later to find our childhood playground had been washed away; the caravans battered and overturned, houses reduced to rubble, and the scene still one of utter desolation. No more hide and seek in the sandhills – they no longer existed. No more playing quoits on king-cup spattered meadows – the meadows were buried beneath mud and debris. It was a traumatic moment; the end of that period of childhood innocence in which one believes that favourite people and places are indestructible.

Like so many others in the country, my father bought a television in time for the Coronation. Today, when even the royal family has no secrets, it's strange to think that in 1953 neither the Archbishop of Canterbury nor the Earl Marshal wanted the Coronation to be shown on television before what they clearly considered to be the vulgar gaze of Her Majesty's loyal subjects. It was Winston Churchill who insisted that television cameras be allowed into Westminster Abbey. Two million cheered the Queen in the streets of London. Over twenty million (some 56% of the adult population) watched on television.

We spent a somewhat cramped and claustrophobic day; family

and friends huddled around the set, keeping our energy up with gallons of tea and vast quantities of sandwiches, pork pies and fruit cake. Although aware, from the weeks of excited build up, the purchase of red white and blue Union Jacks and Coronation Mugs, that we were witness to a momentous occasion, nevertheless the interminable processions turned it into something of an endurance test. Black and white couldn't do justice to the astonishing colour and variety of the uniforms and national costumes of the innumerable nations represented.

The weather, in typically British fashion, put a damper on the day. The rain was so intense that, in Nettleham, a number of people who didn't have cars were caught in a cloudburst on their way to celebrations in the village institute. They had to beat a hasty, sodden retreat and missed the party.

An old photograph shows a Nettleham Coronation football match: men versus women; the men, somewhat self-concious in felt hats, floral dresses and bloomers, looking more like Les Dawson in drag than Danny La Rue. The women won: 5-4.

The Coronation provided me with another opportunity to fill scrapbooks until they bulged with coaches and glittering crowns. My little sister revelled in the children's programmes on our new television. Parents didn't need to ration viewing in those days as the BBC only transmitted for a limited number of hours each day.

Muffin the Mule had first appeared on BBC television in 1946 and was probably its first real star. Every Sunday afternoon at five o'clock he could be found on top of Annette Mills' grand piano together with his friends: Peregrine the Penguin, Oswald the Ostrich, Louise the Lamb. They soon became household names as, before long, did Andy Pandy. When Bill and Ben, the Flowerpot Men, hit the screen our house, like so many, resounded to the constant repetition of 'Oh glubbaglub' and 'Weeeeed'!

But those cuddly creatures on top of the grand piano were in stark contrast to the sad ones in our country lanes, for myxomatosis had struck in 1953 and in some parts of the country would wipe out almost the entire wild rabbit population within the next two years. Coming home in the evenings from the cinema or

26.

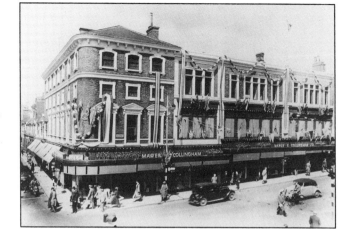

12. *Mawer and Collingham Bedecked for the Coronation 1953*

13. *Nettleham village green in the early nineteen fifties*

14. *The Nettleham Coronation Football Match*

27.

one of our happy sea-side jaunts, we would suddenly feel the car swerve as yet another virus-stricken rabbit was caught in the headlights and my father, wanting to put it quickly out of its misery, deliberately ran it over.

When the infamous *Quatermass Experiment* was shown and terrified half the adult population of Britain, we were smartly marched off to bed before it began. Voracious readers, Jill and I were perfectly happy to read *The Famous Five* and *Swallows and Amazons* until mother came up to kiss us goodnight, her eyes wild and face a delicate shade of green. As the grown-ups' sleep was disturbed by televison-induced nightmares, we fell happily asleep to dream of pirates and hidden treasure.

It was that year that my little sister saved her pocket money for the first time to buy Christmas presents for us. Christmas filled her with such keen anticipation that she bought her gifts – small bars of Cadbury's chocolate – sometime in October. She wrapped them up and hid them gleefully in the dark and dank cupboard beneath the stairs. Periodically she would take them out again (we were aware of, but kept, her secret) and would gloatingly unwrap them and wrap them up again, savouring her 'surprise'. Finally, when the wrapping paper was beginning to fall apart, she left them in peace for a month. There were tears on Christmas Day when Jill fetched them from the cupboard and handed over the poignant tooth-marked remains the mice had not had time to eat.

After comforting my sister, my mother was soon in need of comfort herself when Jill brightened up on receiving my present to her – a shoe box filled with practical jokes. In those days there was a musty and chaotic wonderland of a small shop at the bottom of Steep Hill which sold jokes, colourful paper decorations and favours for parties. Over a number of months, whenever I was in Lincoln, I'd pop in and buy something to add to the collection.

The jokes soon wore thin as far as my parents were concerned, when my sister terrorised them with a pair of hideous fangs, plastic spiders in freshly poured cups of tea, itching powder and a rubber hard-boiled egg. The only thing which met with their approval was a packet of delicate Japanese paper flowers which bloomed, magically, when placed in water.

My mother was a keen amateur thespian and ran the Parent Teachers' Drama Society for many years. The weeks prior to a production saw no peace in the house. We tried desperately to keep out of Mother's way for, if she caught sight of us, a copy of the play in its all too familiar Samuel French cover would be thrust into our unwilling hands. We'd be forced to stand beside the sink as Mother peeled potatoes, and listen again and again to her lines which were accompanied by much gesturing with the potato in one hand and the peeler in the other.

She was keen to instil professional attitudes into her cast but thought nothing of having her own script propped up against something on stage during a performance. But then, as she explained heatedly, she had the whole weight of the production on her shoulders; she was stage manager, actress, director. How could she find time to learn her lines. If we'd been more loyal and willing to hear them instead of hiding under the bed or shinning up the nearest tree . . . it was all too much . . . she was exhausted . . . she'd never do it again . . . . 'Not until the next time,' father would mutter tolerantly.

At the age of eight I was persuaded to tread the boards, or rather springy planks, precariously laid across trestles in the village institute; the footlights, made by John Webster, ingeniously placed in war-time dried milk cans. In one production – *Freckles* – I played the title role. At some point in the convoluted plot I had to pretend to be a black girl – Salamander Savannah. On the last night we ran out of burnt cork. Mrs Webster substituted I knew not what in the heat of the moment. It was some weeks before the Cherry Blossom boot polish faded from my face and I lost my grotesque grey pallor.

Nurse Heath, always a law unto herself, was a member of the cast and incapable of taking direction. She would get on stage and say exactly what she felt like saying, which may have been highly entertaining in itself but played merry havoc with dialogue cues and left other members of the cast open-mouthed in confusion.

15. *Nettleham Teachers/Parents drama group*

16. *Scout Gala Fancy dress party*

30.

During school holidays I had my own drama group in the empty pigsty at the top of the garden. The young audience sat on dusty rugs on the earth floor; the dramatic scenes conducted through an all-pervading odour of manure. My sister, Jill, always intensely loyal, was forced by me to dance a particularly revolting dying swan on her points. In the absence of ballet shoes she balanced daily for a week on the tips of her bunny-bobtail slippers. She hobbled for the rest of the school holidays.

It was during this bunny-bobtail summer that Jill decided to leave home, perhaps thinking it wise to get out before she was permanently crippled by family dramas.

We were alerted by a kindly neighbour who had seen a somewhat forlorn but grimly determined little figure waiting at the bus stop. As Trott's bus puffed and wheezed across the church bridge, my mother rushed out to bring back the runaway. Jill had a teddy bear and a book wrapped in a red and white spotted handkerchief she'd found in the dressing-up box, all tied to the end of a peastick resting on her shoulder. She had seen *Dick Whittington* the previous Christmas.

My mother was for ever spouting poetry: 'Dooo yoooo remember an innnn, Miranda, Doooo you remember an innn. . .' and all those 'beeze that teezed in the high Pyraneez and wine that tasted like a song . . .'

Jill and I puzzled for a long time about how a song tasted. Singing, however, was one of the many things we couldn't do – not that we didn't try, frequently and loudly, with much enthusiasm. What we lacked in tone we made up for in volume – as my poor long-suffering father frequently complained.

My favourite time for singing was when I was tucked up in bed with my sister. We shared a large double bed so high that, when Jill was a toddler, I had to take a flying leap onto the bed and then haul her up onto it. Having read the story of the *Princess and the Pea* we kept half-a-dozen dried peas under the mattress but never felt a thing.

We would lie awake for a long time, despite periodic warnings from our parents, and I would sing to Jill. The songs which moved her greatly, sometimes even to tears, were renderings such as 'Stardust', 'Mate O'Mine', and 'My Mother's Eyes', all learned at my mother's knee. They were delivered in an excrutiatingly high-pitched soprano voice as I felt that the higher I sang the more like an opera singer I would sound. My finale was always a song called 'An Old Violin': 'Up in a garret, Away from the din . . .' which was most inappropriate in view of my squalling. It ended with an exceedingly high note and just before I reached this climax I would feel Jill stiffen as I readied myself for the attempt. I can't think now how my little sister bore it but at the time she fondly and generously believed I could do no wrong, and my efforts used to affect her in a highly emotional way which I found immensely satisfying.

It was about this time that mother decided we should begin our musical education. Perhaps as a result of overhearing my nightly serenades, she decided that if I wasn't to remain tone deaf and my sister made stone deaf, that something would have to be done – fast.

We were sent to the village music mistress, Mrs Gabriel Dickens, daughter of the Reverend Cotton-Smith, a former vicar of Nettleham. Mrs. Dickens, whom we affectionately nicknamed 'Dicky Bird', succoured us with cups of hot Bovril on the winter days when we arrived on her doorstep with fingers too cold to function. Our piano lessons were three guineas a term.

Winter evenings, returning home in the gloom after my lesson, I would hurtle down Washdyke Hill, past the cottages at the bottom of Greetwell Lane, past the lights outside the White Hart pub, dodging vampires disguised as trees.

During the first few months of my music lessons I worked enthusiastically at my set pieces but I became impatiently frustrated by the appalling contrast between my careful plonking and my fantasies of appearing on a concert platform wearing a taffeta ballgown, my virtuoso performance greeted by raptuous applause.

This was fuelled one afternoon when I listened enthralled to 'Sparky and his Magic Piano' played on Aunt Dodo's gleaming radiogram. Sparky, equally frustrated by his plonking, hears his piano talking to him, telling him to place his hands on the keys and to 'go with the flow'. And, wonder of wonders, the notes pour out in an unbroken stream of lyricism; Sparky chuckling with delight at his astonishing performance. Reality returns with a sickening thud when his mother, chiding him for falling asleep at his piano practice, wakes him from his dream.

Mrs. Dickens was an excellent teacher of dauntingly high standards and a degree of endearing eccentricity. She was firmly of the opinion that no composers except The Three B's: Bach, Beethoven and Brahms, were even worthy of mention let alone performance.

When Jill taught herself to play a piece by Offenbach and proudly played it to Mrs. Dickens, she listened patiently before delivering her opinion: 'But never forget that that is not *real* pianoforte music, Elizabeth'. Calling my sister 'Elizabeth', when everyone else called her Jill, was another of her eccentricities.

Her rigid attitude towards what was real music and what was not didn't convince me. My father, who was not at all musical, was delighted when I played 'swing' as he inaccurately called it. I became adept at this and composed a song called *Midnight and Moonlight* ('That's the time I want to hold my baby tight'). My father would greet my all too frequent performances of this hideous noise and much thumping of the piano keys with a look of amazed pride on his face and a rather unrhythmic snapping of his fingers.

My sister's loyalty to Mrs. Dickens, whom she feared would not give my big beat thumping the title of music of *any* kind, made her view all this with less than father's enthusiasm. As soon as I left the piano she would move, in what she hoped was a dignified manner, to take my place and proceed to practice her classical set pieces in her own painstaking way. This would, of course, instantly drive my father out of the room.

But mother would take his place to listen with a far away smile on her face, waving her hand in time to the music and humming softly out of tune. Our music teacher would have disapproved of this kind of humming and mooing along with the music, but my sister could never bring herself to reprove Mother since she was the only one who ever listened to her playing.

My sister became a very talented classical pianist, and still plays to this day, whilst I am reduced to hammering out Chopsticks. I managed to reach my teens before someone less loyal and more honest with me than my sister shattered my belief that I had a beautiful voice. I joined the choir at the High School and we made a record: *Mists Before the Sunrise Fly.* During the numerous recording takes a pipingly flat voice could be heard through the saccharine unity of the other voices. It was mine. I was chucked out of the choir.

5.

ACH WINTER THERE WOULD BE healthy treks to Riseholme, muffled up in our scarves, to pick snowdrops in the grounds of Nettleham Hall; a gaunt country mansion long since burned out. The blackened walls crazy-paved with cracks, and the bleak window sockets dared us closer; the snap, crackle, and pop of twigs signalled nerves failing. Clutching snowdrops in now sticky palms we scampered back to the safety of the farm workers' cottages taking furtive little backward glances until we reached the corner of Welton Road and could stop for deep, relieved gulps of frosty air.

We tramped the Welton Road to the woods to sniff the ground like truffle hunters to uncover the first violets of spring. We returned home, smelling the sweet and all pervading scent of the violets, guilty feelings surfacing when our tiny and delicate fistfuls wilted almost beyond revival before being handed over to mother.

When, one summer, despite her misgivings, I was allowed to have a two-wheeled bicycle, I pedalled furiously to keep up with my twin cousins, John and Michael. With picnics of Dandelion and Burdock, Tizer, egg sandwiches and jam tarts packed into saddle bags, we set out eagerly to explore the outposts of our world: Sudbrooke, Dunholme, Welton. We tried to locate, with stealth and trepidation, the hermit who was rumoured to live in a little hut deep in Sudbrooke Woods. We picked cowslips, and in autumn scoured hedges for blackberries, triumphantly returning home with scratched, stained fingers, fruit for pies and stomach-ache. Unaccompanied by adults, able to wander as we chose, gave the world an added lustre. The flatness of Lincolnshire enhanced our sense of liberation. With no high hills or mountains to mark a boundary and impede our progress, we felt we could have cycled on and on until we dropped off the edge of the world.

If only little legs could have kept up with such a fantasy. On one memorable day – unbeknownst to mother – we biked to

Fiskerton. I could hardly walk on my return and spent the next day reeling around drunkenly like a midget cowboy.

We stopped and explored deserted airfields. The sadly cracking runways overgrown with weeds, the decrepit Nissen huts with broken windows and peeling paint, the now empty control tower watching like a benevolent sentinel, were poignant reminders of the young war-time airmen and the insecurity of their lives. Growing up in close proximity to Scampton we were proudly aware of their deeds.

When the *Dam Busters* film was made in the early fifties, and the stars and crew came to Scampton and Hemswell to shoot scenes, we were drunk with excitement. On trips to Lincoln with mother, we invented excuses for visiting the Bail where the star, Richard Todd, who played Guy Gibson, was staying at The White Hart Hotel. Sidling nonchalantly past, we longed for a glimpse of him. I persuaded mother to buy me the sheet music of the *Dam Busters* theme tune from Bill Rose's music shop at the corner of Tentercroft Street. It didn't sound quite so stirring when picked out on the piano.

We poured into the cinema in droves on the film's release to see our local heroes. We found their deeds much more romantically awesome than the adventures of Dan Dare in the Eagle comic. What we couldn't quite square with our heroic visions, however, was the sight of Guy Gibson's former batman, Mr. Crosby – known as 'Bing' – amiable and bespectacled and now immortalised on film, riding around Nettleham where he lived – on a *bicycle*. With the RAF motto *Per Ardua ad Astra* – 'Through Endeavour to the Stars' ringing in our ears but unaware at that age of the British quality of modest understatement, we found this much too down to earth.

In 1954, the year the country celebrated the end of food rationing and Roger Bannister's achievement in running a four-minute mile, I was celebrating my acceptance by Christ's Hospital High School for Girls. I was part of the post-war bulge; an intake of ninety new girls who formed almost a quarter of the total roll of 380 pupils. We were the ones who would benefit from the

17. Christ's Hospital School for Girls – Lincoln

18. Greestone stairs

19. The long-suffering
cooks and dinner-ladies
at the High School

37.

Education Act of 1944 which had made it compulsory for Local Authorities to provide free secondary education for all pupils up to a minimum age of fifteen.

The school had an excellent and deserved reputation for academic excellence and was initially daunting for a new girl. After the small, cosy complex of Nettleham Infants and Junior School, I was overwhelmed by its size and seeming grandeur. At that time it was housed on Greestone Stairs in what is now the Art College in Lincoln. Gold-lettered boards in the panelled assembly hall listed the names of illustrious former pupils who had gained university places. The school magazine provided news each year of Old Girls who were working in leper colonies, up the Orinoco without a paddle, or pouring over medieval madrigals at weekend music festivals. The school was also twinned with one in Tours, France, in that magical place: 'abroad'.

In winter we wore navy skirts, green aertex shirts and green V-necked pullovers, blue ties and sensible regulation shoes. In summer, cotton dresses which were shapeless, creased badly, and were allowed only in a limited choice of washed-out pastel colours. I was very proud of my school blazer with its badge but hated the navy serge hats which were stiff and unflattering; much more flattering when the fashion-conscious softened them up a bit by bashing them repeatedly against the cloakroom wall. It was forbidden to write with anything other than an Osmiroid fountain pen with a regulation nib. My fingers were soon permanently inkstained.

Whenever I think of my early days at the High School I recall with envy a remark made by a certain Emperor Sigismund who lived during the 14th century. When his tutor, criticising him for his poor Latin, said he should try harder, Sigismund was royally annoyed: 'I am the Roman Emperor,' he retorted haughtily, 'and I am above grammar.' I wish after complaints about my howlers that I'd been able to 'do a Sigismund'.

I don't know who said schooldays are the happiest of your life but I imagine it must have been the original school swot who wandered happily around, piled up to the chin with text books,

20. The High School hall before the platform was built at the other end

21. A view of the other end of the hall from the gallery after the platform had been built

22. Chemistry 'Stink-bombs' lab at the High School

only putting them down to leap onto the platform at prizegiving to receive more.

Perhaps some of us do think they were the happiest days because we remember only the good times and forget those agonising examinations when the mind was as blank as the paper, the hours with clenched fists beating foreheads trying to assimilate declensions, or those occasions when a compass produced only bloody pricked fingers and egg-shaped circles. I found algebraic equations so inexplicable that even on the occasions when I did get the answers right I still found them so inexplicable that I didn't know how I'd done it.

Miss Cleave, the headmistress, had been appointed in 1943 at the age of thirty-eight from eighty-nine candidates. She had been Head of Modern Languages at Cheltenham Ladies College. It was noticeable. We were expected to behave like young ladies; although the discipline was tempered with a deep understanding. She was highly respected.

Academic excellence was expected and was to be underpinned by moral rectitude. At my first school Speech Day we were addressed by Mrs. Seely, an Old Girl of the school, ex-headmistress of Mount Street Primary School, wife of the vice-chairman of our governing body and a former mayoress of Lincoln. She spoke of 'Airs on a G. String.'

She suggested that many important qualities began with the letter G. Gratitude – for a place at a grammar school and for other blessings such as good parents and good health; of a need to express this gratitude. Making use of these blessings required Grit – which helped us to get a firm grasp on our work and wrestle with difficulties. It also helped us to obey our consciences; a discipline which was essential for living our lives as we ought. Finally, on her string of G's, Mrs Seely found Generosity. One of the noblest qualities in the world. It helped us to give of ourselves to others in return for the blessings showered upon us. Heady stuff for eleven year olds, but never forgotten.

Marriage was stoically accepted as a fairly normal occurrence for a girl but preferably after she had succeeded at something else

, or planned to continue with a career after marriage. Domestic Science was given a token glance: a few periods of dusting, learning to make hospital corners on a bed (Mrs. Bursey would never have approved of duvets), and stuffing a couple of tomatoes which I bore home in messy triumph squashed against text books in my overloaded satchel. In my first year I was so thrilled at being a Christ's Hospital School girl that I dragged home far more books than I needed for homework, just so that I could show them to my parents. My skinny shoulder was soon rubbed raw and I was in danger of becoming lop-sided.

Sport left me cold, particularly during the winter months when we had to go up to the sports field on Nettleham Road. Navy knickers, hockey sticks, bouncing breasts when I was still only The Shape of Things to Come, pubescent perspiration and freezing changing rooms, filled me with unalloyed agony. I always seemed to arrive at the hurdles one stride short or one too many and could never see the point of bruised shins to win a tarnished hockey cup. I prayed for rain on the days we were expected to be out on the sports field.

But when English compositions had to be written for homework, or contributions were invited for the school magazine, I was eager to start. I'd rush down Lindum Hill, my satchel bouncing against my hip, leap on to Trott's bus in Unity Square and on the journey home happily contemplate an evening writing my description of Skegness in winter: 'The gnomes, with their faded paint, stared gloomily into the drained lily pond in the deserted ornamental gardens, longing for summer to begin . . . '

Summer holidays meant set books which I always looked forward to reading – books such as Thomas Hardy's *The Trumpet Major*, and Charles Dickens' *Great Expectations* which introduced me to the good-hearted, gentle Joe Gargery and his 'What larks, eh Pip!' and 'On the Rampage, Pip, and off the Rampage, Pip; such is Life!'

Our early sex education consisted of a number of lectures given in the school library by a visiting lady doctor with a moustache. These talks took place in an atmosphere of strained silence. The doctor was a trifle taken aback when, during question time, Frederika Huckle asked if monkeys had periods.

Thanks, unwittingly, to my mother, my form was already rather blasé on the subject of sex. When Mother learned that I would be studying biology she helpfully gave me a book which she'd bought at a Nettleham jumble sale. Flicking through the first few pages at her usual speed she'd noted it was about birds, bees, and frogs. If she'd flicked a bit further she'd have learned, to her consternation, that it was also about human biology and sexuality – in some considerable and explicit detail. How such a book came to be in a Nettleham jumble sale is still a mystery; there couldn't have been many like it available in the early fifties.

The book, in a brown paper cover on which I'd written 'RICHARD III by William Shakespeare', went round the class. Having absorbed its contents we cheerfully forgot them. At the age of eleven we had much more interesting things to think about – like making stink bombs in the chemistry lab.

Although I subsequently returned it – minus its Shakespeare cover – to the shelves in the bedroom which I shared with my sister, I learned, many years later, that she'd never bothered to open it. In the fifties, the Bob Hope 'Road' films – *Road to Bali*, *Road to Morocco* – were popular. Glancing at the title: *The Road to Maturity*, Jill had assumed it was something to do with Bob Hope and thus of no interest to her.

6.

METEOROLOGISTS TEND TO DISMISS as collective amnesia the commonly-held belief that the weather was different in childhood and, logically, if each generation says the same, then the weather men must be right. And yet I'm still convinced that the seasons when I was growing up in the fifties were more clearly defined than they are today; that the summers were hotter and the winters colder.

January 1954 produced weather of such Arctic temperatures that Europe almost ground to a standstill. Two years later, the 1st February 1956, was the coldest day since 1895. I can't believe that it is only in my imagination that I see my grandfather, who had made me a beautiful streamlined sledge, bringing it out of storage each year to oil and polish the runners until they gleamed.

As soon as the first flakes started to fall in that strange, eery stillness that seems to accompany snow, I'd stand by the window willing the flakes to settle. The best times were those when, on waking and drawing back the curtains, I discovered with gasps of delight that it had secretly snowed during the night. After gulping down a warming breakfast of bacon and eggs and fried bread, I'd shift impatiently from foot to foot as mother checked that my coat and scarf, gloves and woolly hat, thick socks and wellie boots would provide sufficient insulation. I dragged my sledge out into the High Street, eager to be off. There I'd see lots of other figures, like diminutive characters in a Lowry painting, some pausing gleefully to throw snowballs, all ultimately converging on the nursery slopes of Nettleham village park near the bottom of Mill Hill.

It would take a few painful practice runs before the reflexes, sluggish from remaining unused since the previous winter, began to work again. Soon, however, I'd remember how to judge accurately when to brake with my heels and so wouldn't have to fling myself off the sledge to avoid shooting like greased lightning into the hedge which bordered the bottom of the slope opposite the vicarage garden.

One year Jill and I, together with Patty and Jenny Phillips who were friends and neighbours, built a gigantic snowman and an igloo. We spent hours shaping and cutting the blocks of snow. Lacking the Eskimo's innate talent for such things ours, although large enough to crawl inside, was more Cubist than smooth-domed. It must have been bitterly cold *that* winter for the igloo remained intact for many days.

We spent many happy Christmases with Aunt Maud, Uncle John and cousin Richard at their home which was in one of the streets running down from Monks Road in Lincoln. Aunt Maud had, and still has in her eighties, a beautiful, pure soprano voice which was often heard at concerts in Lincoln both before and after the war. It can still be heard today when she sings solos with a choir in Sutton-on-Sea. At our family Christmases she did her full-bosomed thrush routine standing beside the piano: 'The Lost Chord', 'The Holy City', 'Ave Maria'. She also led our enthusiastic, 'though far from tuneful, carol singing.

After an hour of this, however, we usually decided it was time for something more raucous and demanded charades. We looked on with unconcealed delight as mother, having drunk Pimms as innocently as fruit cup, draped herself in a curtain and acted out her scene as if her life depended on it, accidentally lobbing a chrysanthemum into Aunt Maud's eye. Her mimes were rivetingly dramatic but rarely had much to do with the word she was supposedly trying to illustrate. This she would hotly deny when we all yelled in fury having failed to guess the word and she told us what it was. None of us is ever likely to forget her attempt to portray *The Birth of a Nation*.

In fairness to my mother, she wasn't solely responsible for this. Uncle John was somewhat liberal handed when mixing drinks. Matters came to a head one Christmas when Aunt Maud, peeling potatoes for Christmas dinner and having drunk but a single cocktail, was somewhat startled to discover she'd calmly tipped all the potatoes into the dustbin and put the peelings on to boil. Uncle John's cocktail-shaking generosity was abruptly curbed.

We never tired of charades and guessing games: 'Knock, knock, Who's there?' we'd yell. 'I don't care if it's King Kong,' replied father, wearily, 'It's bedtime.' Aunt Maud, immediately taking this as her cue, would launch herself, with the faintest touch of affectionate irony, into the song: *The End of a Perfect Day*. As Richard, Jill and I, still not convinced that it should end, climbed the stairs to bed, her voice would follow us. . .'For memory has painted that perfect day, in colours that never fade . . .'

Although we'd been told to go to bed we hadn't been told to put out the light. As the adults below enjoyed a nightcap free of our demands, we eagerly devoured our Christmas books and Eagle and Girl annuals. But one year I found a book belonging to Uncle John: *The Scourge of the Swastika*. I was ill-prepared for it. In a heightened state of shock I read of the incomprehensible horrors of the concentration camps and the extent of the evil which Britain had fought against during the war. In the midst of our festivities, it was a painfully sobering experience.

So also, on an obviously very different level, was reading in 1955 that Ruth Ellis had been found guilty of murder. She was the last woman to be hanged in Britain. I remember this well because my mother had known the man Ruth Ellis shot and killed when he was still a small boy in Sheffield.

The hanging, particularly of a woman, led to a heated debate in the country on capital punishment and the desire for a referendum. In the Lincolnshire Chronicle at the time, someone signing herself *Nervous* , wrote:

> 'I hope it is not too late for the British public to register their protest against the rush to abolish hanging for murder. This is an issue which I think should be referred to public referendum. I tremble to think of the brutes who are likely to force their way into our homes either to rob or for lust, and who will stop at nothing to gain their ends. Are we to return to the days when our menfolk carried swords and daggers for self-defence or are we to buy revolvers? This mamby pamby attitude towards murderers and thugs is sickening to say the least and unrealistic in these days of hard materialism.'

'Nervous' didn't get her wish and capital punishment was abolished, but her awareness, even in the fifties, of the rise of 'hard materialism' was astute and prophetic. In Lincolnshire, however, with its dependence upon agriculture, there were more worrying matters closer to home. Hordes of wood pigeons had been ravaging the crops and it was believed they had flown over from Scandinavia. The other correspondent on the Letters Page suggested that they could jolly well fly back home again.

I was born on Christmas Eve, something for which I have never forgiven my parents, resulting as it has in a lifetime of receiving Christmas cards from friends with 'PS Happy Birthday' scrawled on the bottom. But the arctic Christmas of 1955 was memorable for a joint twelfth birthday and Christmas present from my parents – my first record player – a Dansette.

Communal family entertainment was treated with indifference that year. Aunt Maud was given little opportunity to sing those old-fashioned sentimental ballads. When the adults suggested charades or guessing games we wearily suggested they went off somewhere else and amused themselves – quietly. All Richard, Jill and I wanted to do was to play over and over again Bill Haley's 'Rock Around the Clock'. As our parents pleaded with us to 'stop that racket', we were unaware of how profound an impact this recording would have; how it would create a dividing line between all the music that had come before and would come after it; that Rock and Roll would change popular culture. All we youngsters knew was that we'd never heard music more exciting.

In 1956 the greatest excitement in Nettleham was when the ford on Vicarage Lane, where cars splashed through beside the footbridge, was finally spanned by a road bridge, and in Lincoln when Eddie Calvert, the Man with the Golden Trumpet, Mrs. Shufflewick and Jimmy James appeared live at the Savoy in March.

In July, Colonel Nasser announced the nationalisation of the Suez Canal, threatening to strangle the link with what remained of our Empire. According to Anthony Eden, Prime Minister at the time, the Egyptian president had 'placed his finger on our windpipe'. We joined in the great surge of jingoistic fury which this action provoked in Britain.

Petrol rationing had ended in the spring of 1950 but it was now reimposed during the Suez Crisis. We spent Christmas that year in Bridlington thanks to black market petrol. We stayed in an hotel overlooking the sea and were accompanied by another Nettleham family – the Bavins.

Knowing our predilection for party games and perhaps in need of a rest from us, the adults went out on the town leaving the other rather elderly guests to the tender mercies of my sister Jill, the Bavin's son, Michael, and myself.

I recited the whole of the interminable poem *The Traveller* to the consternation of the other hotel guests and scooped a couple of pounds for fulfilling my forfeit with such boring efficiency. Sadly, it is still one of the few poems I can still remember in its entirety.

As this Christmas was the occasion of my thirteenth birthday, I felt it was time to behave in a grown up manner. I refused to exchange my first pair of high-heeled shoes (very low high heels) for black wellies to tramp the beach with sixteen year old Michael and my eight year old sister.

I sat in the bay window of our hotel bedroom all afternoon watching them throwing stones into the sea below and talking animatedly. I felt, in turn, madly mature and above all that now I was a teenager and sadly certain that they were having much more fun than I was.

7.

I N 1957 WHEN THE RUSSIANS launched a dog into space, many people in Britain ran true to stereotype by being more concerned about the welfare of the dog than thrilled by such a stunning technological advance.

Nettleham's white-hot technological advance was throwing out the Elsans with a sigh of relief when mains drainage belatedly arrived in the village. It must have played havoc with the Lincolnshire water table for a few weeks as Nettleham resounded to the welcome music of constantly flushing lavatories.

In Lincoln, the old Durham Ox public house was demolished together with many old buildings when the construction of the Pelham Bridge cut a swathe through the bottom of Broadgate.

In Nettleham, a thunderbolt cut a swathe through the High Street, smashing windows in homes and shops from as far up the street as the Methodist chapel and as far down as the Junior School. Two of our upstairs windows were blown out in the blast and shattered on the pavement; fortunately not hitting anyone. Television sets, irons and clocks were burned out and the fuses at the two sub-stations of the East Midlands Electricity Board in the village were blown. A motorist, driving down the High Street, felt his car being lifted into the air. I was reading in the sitting room which overlooked the High Street at the time and heard a thunderclap like a bomb blast and saw an orange ball of fire which appeared to explode in the park. The glass merchants and glaziers had a profitable week.

The force of the blast was such that a fragment of the church clock was blown off, fell inside the tower and down through the space through which the bell ropes were suspended. It was later found embedded between the pages of a prayer book; the paper singed where it had come to rest. In more primitive and God-fearing times this would no doubt have been taken as some kind of omen.

Far more worrying later that year, was the polio epidemic which subdued Lincolnshire in August. Scores of people, particularly children, were in hospital and, fearing the spread of the disease, we were actively discouraged from playing together, going to parties or congregating anywhere in groups.. We were given an extra week's holiday from school in the hope that the crisis would pass before term finally began. For once we didn't welcome such an extension as we heard of schoolfriends succumbing to the disease. Isolated within our families, sent to bed early each night by parents who hoped that rest would keep it at bay, we counted the days until life returned to normal.

When it was announced that the Queen would open the new bridge on 27th June 1958 and a number of pupils from the Grammar and Secondary Schools would be chosen to dance before her, I longed to be one of the chosen. It would be an honour and anyway, I liked dancing. I feared, however, that having recently blotted my copybook at the High School I might be passed over.

School lunches, provided in the Tithe Barn on Greestone Stairs, were often greeted with howls of anguish and derision. There never seemed to be enough food, and the quality of the meat, in our opinion, left much to be desired. There were some unseemly arguments between growing girls about the last roast potato and rude remarks about the need for sharpened fangs to chew the meat. When the chorus of criticism became a clamour in my form I found myself unwillingly appointed spokesman. I made an appointment to see the headmistress, Miss Cleave, having secreted in my pocket a piece of meat which I felt would support my complaint.

It was three days before Miss Cleave deigned to give me an audience. I confronted her across her lavender-polished desk on which I had placed the offending bit of gristle now suffering from *rigor mortis* and stuck to my smelly handkerchief. Miss Cleave's astonishing nose for intelligence was so well developed that I realised that not only had she been aware of my reason for wishing to see her but also of my gruesome 'Exhibit Number One'. By keeping me waiting she was able to argue that the specimen I presented could not be described as a 'fair' and 'true' example of the quality of the meat. She taught me a useful lesson in tactics – and in forgiveness. She held no grudges. I was chosen to dance before the Queen.

I didn't, of course. After our weeks of painstaking rehearsal, British weather, which has no sense of occasion, rained the dancing off. We cheered the Queen from the bleak stands as she was driven around the soggy football pitch beneath a grey saucepan lid of glowering clouds. What was very annoying, having been denied my moment of glory, was seeing the photograph of the opening of the bridge published in the Echo. Standing on the front row, waving Union Jacks, were Graham Hindle and my sister.

The Queen was soon forgotten and the photographs of her in the Lincolnshire Echo and Chronicle did not tempt me to bring out my scissors and Royal scrapbooks; they'd been pushed unceremoniously into the bottom of my bedroom cupboard after the Coronation. Now fifteen, my interests lay, like so many of my contemporaries, in clothes and Rock and Roll. Our parents despaired of us.

Skiffle was soon dismissed as folksie tunes for the home-knitted pullover brigade when we were bombarded by the raw seductive sounds pouring out of America. One or two of our friends had a Saturday job at Spouge's in the Cornhill and were the envy of all.

Spouge's, which had moved to the Cornhill in 1926, sold gramophones, radios, televisions and lighting. They opened a record department which became a meeting place on Saturday afternoons for Lincoln's adolescents and a magnet for our pocket money. We squeezed into the listening booths to hear the latest releases before the agonising moment when, realising our pocket money would only stretch so far, we had to choose between Connie Francis or the Everly Brothers' songs of innocence and experience. At the High School the choir, of which I was a member, cut a record: *Mists before The Sunrise Fly.* It didn't have much chance of making the top ten.

Valentine, the Mills and Boon of girls' romantic magazines, disapproved of by our school mistresses, was kept hidden in our

23. A view of the crowd at the opening of
The Pelham Bridge 27th June 1958

24. A small section of the crowd at the opening
of the Pelham Bridge

satchels and furtively read during milk break in the school gardens which ran behind the Usher Art Gallery. One week the magazine offered a special recording of Elvis Presley talking to his fans: 'Hi, this is Elvis Presley . . .' I lay on my bed one Sunday morning playing it over and over again until my mother finally lost patience.

We slapped on the smelly Amami and tried out new hairstyles, sticking kiss-curls on to our foreheads like Bill Haley. We soaked our full petticoats in sugar to make them stiff, overlaid them with colourful dirndl skirts, waists tightly cinched by cummerbunds and went to dances in the Co-operative Hall looking like pegtops. It was impossible to sit down in such skirts with any semblance of grace. By the end of the evening, after hours of dancing or standing in stiletto-heeled winklepickers, we would stagger out to meet our long-suffering fathers waiting patiently to collect us in the family cars, our legs inelegantly splayed, our feet throbbing.

Cranwell cadets frequently attended the dances and some of them turned green after a few beers. It never failed to astonish us that the boys who were least able to hold their liquor or to keep their cars on the road – there was often a battered sports car in the ditch near Sleaford – somehow managed to stay up in the air without mishap. We also found it curious that the manners of our boyfriends from the Lincoln Grammar and City Schools so often put those of the Cranwell cadets – many of them from public schools – to shame.

When parents insisted it was time that we turned off the record player and got some fresh air, we played tennis on the old weed-covered courts at the top of Mill Hill in Nettleham. The net was so ragged that a frequent call was: 'Did that go over or through?' Our mothers tried to keep their figures in trim by attending the Keep Fit class in the village institute. An early forerunner of Jane Fonda and her aerobics, it was far less self-concious. There were no glamorous lycra work-out suits; the women huffing and puffing in baggy old trousers and plimsolls.

My mother returned one evening from Keep Fit and announced, somewhat shamefacedly but finding it difficult to hide her amusement, that she'd been banned. Some weeks before, the instructress had sent her to the back row because her vocally exuberant but totally unco-ordinated physical jerks were distracting the class. This evening, however, she had Gone Too Far. She'd swung her hula-hoop with such force that it had caught on the metal hat peg on the wall behind her and hung her up; understandably causing uproar.

Sadly, during term time, Christ's Hospital School for Girls continued to expect what I increasingly felt was far too much of my time. I enjoyed my art lessons, for Miss Oyler was an inspiring art teacher, and pinning dead frogs to boards for dissection. I felt a lump in my throat whenever the entire school took a deep, collective breath in the cathedral on Commemoration Day and launched themselves into the school song *Jerusalem* .

I was a timid but willing participant in the end-of-term rag when we turned all the pictures in the corridors (including a bad reproduction of Van Gogh's *Sunflowers*) to the wall and chalked FRYING TONIGHT on a stolen blackboard which we placed by the entrance to the school. This could be seen by a steady stream of traffic groaning up Lindum Hill.

But I was fed up with subjects requiring more serious attention to study and homework and the looming prospects of sitting GCE examinations. It was comforting to know that I wasn't the only one who felt like that in my year.

With that lethargy peculiar to adolescence when asked to do something one does not wish to do, we groaned inwardly at the sight of the gym mistress bouncing with health, perfect of deportment, iron of discipline. We could never see how we could possibly benefit from shinning up ropes to a dangerous height or throwing ourselves with reckless abandon into elevated splits over hurdles.

To our surprise, the headmistress seemed to possess an extraordinary understanding of the growing pains and interests of teenage girls. One morning she announced in assembly that Mawer and Collingham would present a fashion show at the school. A number of sixth form girls would be chosen to model the clothes.

Mawer and Collingham had been founded in 1820 by Mr. Mawer and Mr. Collingham. I always imagined them as sober-suited gentlemen, with wing collars and watch chains, peering benevolently over half-moon spectacles, smelling astringently of gentlemen's cologne. It was the epitome of a small and gracious department store. Sad to think that such former glory has now been buried under the dreary name of Binns, as the exterior has been buried under a faceless modern cladding.

County ladies wearing gloves, hats and well-cut tweed suits, met for tea or coffee in the upstairs tea-room after selecting an evening dress for a County Ball, a pair of fully-fashioned stockings or being discreetly measured for a new corset. With its hushed atmosphere and genteel displays, the store represented for many years old-fashioned ideas of quality and dignity. Such virtues didn't appeal to us. We didn't think much of a store which displayed passport photographs in one window, or in which we were terrified of turning into proverbial bulls when a bulging school satchel sent a piece of porcelain flying in the china department.

We were eager for cheap, 'with it', youthful fashions. After the initial excitement at the idea of a fashion show, we assumed it would consist of the kind of conservative, lady-like dresses towards which mothers still tried to steer their daughters in the store.

Our mistake. The then managing director at Mawer and Collingham chose the clothes with care from the top fashion houses, including a couple of deep violet Cardin wool coats from Paris. I was one of the fortunate ones selected to model them. Trying on the clothes, with their exquisitely finished seams, perfect cut and superb fabrics, we instinctively moved gracefully and, although we hated to admit it, knew we were enhanced by them.

The highlight, for me, was sweeping down the staircase onto the school stage trailing a mink along the floor behind me. Whether or not we would be able to afford such clothes later in our lives, it was a timely lesson in style and quality.

8.

A LTHOUGH AN INCREASING AMOUNT of free time was now spent
with schoolfriends and boyfriends, my parents, sister and I
still continued to do many things together as a family;
friends frequently included. My parents were extremely generous
and hospitable but there must have been times when my father,
sitting down to a meal and finding himself surrounded by yet more
strange faces, must have wondered whether he was destined to
feed the entire teenage population of Lincolnshire. He never knew
in advance who would be joining us for a Sunday excursion and
occasionally, seeing yet another body squeezing into the back seat
of the car, clutching a swimming costume or camera, he'd turn to
me and whisper: 'Who's this one?'

Throughout the fifties we spent many weekends, both summer
and winter, on the Lincolnshire coast although after the floods the
formerly peaceful scene changed. We had now reached an age
when such changes were welcome, and long walks along the beach
were happily replaced by the jukebox, the slot machine, and clock
golf.

We were eager participants in car treasure hunts which
suddenly became immensely popular at that time. On summer
evenings we met up with all the other car loads, including our
friends the Hindle, West and Phillips families, either on the village
green or outside the White Hart pub in Nettleham. Opening the
first clue we shouted urgent contradictory instructions to my
bewildered father, who once drove round and round in circles in
an attempt to show us up while we tried to come to some
agreement about the direction we should take.

Scothern residents were roused from their suppers;
bewildered people in Saxilby discovered strangers who had
misinterpreted clues tramping across their gardens; dramatic U-
turns were made when we spotted someone we thought might be
on the right track heading in the opposite direction. Dust was

raised in attics in pursuit of a pith-helmet or a stone hot-water bottle. Grannies were left standing on doorsteps whimpering pathetically: 'Don't let anyone know it's mine!' as they unwillingly surrendered a cracked old chamber pot.

We explored Tattershall Castle and the ruins of Fountains Abbey. We had tea at Woodhall Spa and visited the Kinema in the Woods. At Manchester Zoo we staggered out of the camel house overcome by the smell. We roamed around London, Cambridge, Filey, the Yorkshire Moors and the wonderful museum at York. We trooped around stately homes. At Chatsworth House we pretended not to know Aunt Maud who, when trying to take some rhododendrons home furtively hidden in a travelling rug, was exposed when she accidentally dropped the rug and it opened in the busy car park.

My sister, who had reached that peculiar age when horses are preferable to people, became a trifle bored with all these cultural excursions. So, as a concession to her, we went to the Easter races at Market Rasen. Having gone through the card by some lucky fluke and supplemented our pocket money by fourteen shillings, we watched in horror as a jockey was thrown heavily from his horse in the last race. My mother, fearing terrible injuries to the jockey, was too distracted to notice that my sister had left her side and rushed through the crowds. Suddenly spotting her running down the course, my mother set off in pursuit. Arriving breathless, she was greeted by my sister saying consolingly: 'Don't worry, Mummy, the horse is going to be alright.'

Trying to leave after the meeting was slow and laborious as streams of cars converged into a single exit. In front of us was a clapped out old banger, its back seat packed with enough children of various shapes and ages to win one of those 'How many can be crammed into a car?' competitions. It waited meekly to be let in as the smarter Jaguars and Rovers ignored it. Finally, a determined little woman leapt from the front passenger seat, ran into the oncoming traffic and imperiously held up her arm. In the stillness that followed she waved her husband and brood forward. ı

I didn't realise, at that time, that Market Rasen, a small town in Lincolnshire, had played such a significant part in the life of the writer – James Joyce. Desperate to leave Ireland in his youth, Joyce combed the Dublin newspapers for job advertisements and, among others, replied to one placed by the Midland Scholastic Agency in Market Rasen. It was asking for English teachers to work on the continent. In September 1904 Joyce received a reply from a Miss Gilford at the agency in Market Rasen. She confirmed that a position had been reserved for him as an English teacher in a Berlitz school, but refused to send him full particulars until he sent her two guineas; a considerable sum of money in those days.

Joyce, having contacted officials in Market Rasen and received an assurance that Miss Gilford was a trustworthy local lady, sent the two guineas. At the beginning of October he heard once again from Miss Gilford. Her letter confirmed that his new job was in Zurich, Switzerland.

Although Joyce had received another letter, this one from the Berlitz School in London warning him that it had no agents in the United Kingdom and that he should take care when dealing with supposed agencies, he chose to ignore the warning in his eagerness to leave Ireland with his sweetheart, Nora Barnacle.

The couple left Dublin for Zurich when Joyce was twenty-two and Nora only twenty and the couple lived together until finally marrying in 1931. In Zurich they learned that the Berlitz Director did not have a position for James Joyce and that he had never heard of that shady lady, Miss Gilford, of Market Rasen in Lincolnshire. But a job was found for Joyce, teaching English at a new Berlitz School in Pola, Yugoslavia, and shortly afterwards in Trieste.

And so Joyce and Nora's peripatetic life abroad, including those years in Trieste and Paris, was set in motion by Miss Gilford of Market Rasen; years in which Joyce wrote *The Dubliners*, *Finnegans Wake* and *Ulysses*.

Much as I loved our family outings, I was eager to get away from my parents' watchful eyes and went to London to a conference at which the High School in Lincoln had agreed to participate.

I stayed, with Brenda East, Jean Manners and Valerie Stapleton, at the Regent House Hotel in Bloomsbury. I can't recall now what the conference was about but can remember vividly our visits to the 'Two I's' and 'Heaven and Hell' coffee bars in Old Compton Street, Soho, and the evening we travelled out to the Hackney Empire on the tube to watch a recording of a Bill Maynard television show.

The Seven Wonders of the World in Cinerama, which we also saw, only added to our teenage frustrations at the limited boundaries of our lives. Few of us had ever been abroad. The High School had cultural exchanges with a school in Tours, France, but I had never been allowed to participate.

Each year a group of girls went over to stay with families in France and the daughters were hosted in Lincoln in return. We would eagerly await their arrival at school assembly: the beautifully cut bobbed hair, stylish clothes and precocious elegance. Instinctively feeling provincial when confronted by such sophistication, we revelled in the lurid stories told by High School girls returning from their Tours visit, exaggerated no doubt, of the French girls' more relaxed attitude to 'You Know What' and the yukky food prepared in kitchens greasily coated with olive oil and stinking of garlic.

Other than the French girls and tourists attracted to the glorious Cathedral, there were few foreigners in Lincoln; a city which could never have been described as cosmopolitan. Such foreigners as there were understandably attracted our interest.

One evening, accompanied by a Nigerian apprentice student at Rustons, a group of us came out of the Corn Exchange to find it snowing heavily. The Nigerian started in terror at the snowflakes swirling in the blackness, then rushed back inside, fearful of what was falling from the sky and dissolving on his shoulders.

We were fascinated at the thought that someone had never seen snow before, but would have been reluctant to admit that the world beyond our own was almost equally foreign and outside our experience.

To increase our knowledge, a number of us at school had been invited to correspond with penfriends in Africa. Periodically, blue airmail envelopes would arrive from my penfriend – by coincidence also Nigerian. On one occasion, a massive wooden crate was delivered by a perspiring postman.

When my father, with the help of hammer and chisel, managed to prise open the lid, we were met by an appalling smell and the sight of the forlorn remains of two rotten coconuts. The box had been sent by sea and must have taken months to reach me. Not wanting to disappoint my penfriend, I told him how much we had enjoyed eating them.

The correspondence stopped abruptly on my part, however, when my penfriend sent a photograph of himself: tall, well-built, handsome and in full tribal dress with a pair of very large leather sandals peeking out of his highly patterned cotton robes. He told me that he was the son of a Chieftain and asked that I send him details of my height and vital statistics. He wished to know my measurements for the marriage throne.

9.

L IKE SO MANY OF MY CONTEMPORARIES, I was mad about clothes. We all lived in fear of wearing the same outfit twice. My mother, in whose hand a sewing needle looked as incongruous as a wooden spoon in the hand of a brain surgeon, sent me on a sewing course at the Singer shop, then at the bottom of Steep Hill in Lincoln.

The course lasted for a couple of weeks during the summer holidays and was invaluable; the only problem being that the shop was small and the only place I could practise was at a seat in the window. Or so I was told. I suspect now that having a live dummy on display was useful publicity. Word soon spread and, trying to sew neatly down the lines and around the circles of perforations on my training cards, I would become uncomfortably aware that I was no longer alone. I'd look up to see curious strangers and schoolfriends, their noses firmly pressed against the window, their eyes deliberately crossed, making grotesque faces at me. Pressing the treadle fiercely in my embarrassment, another practise card would shoot from beneath the needle leaving me with a jammed sewing machine and a knot of tangled cotton to unravel.

Thanks to my sewing course and the loan of a machine, I felt confident enough to scour the market in Lincoln each Saturday for remnants which I'd make up to supplement the clothes I could afford to buy from Eve Brown, Dorothy Perkins, or Charles. A pink mohair sweater cost 23/11d, a pair of winklepickers 55/11d.

Many feverish hours were spent hunched over the sewing machine and often I was finishing the hem minutes before leaving for the next dance. On one occasion I discovered, when already in the car, that I'd sewn my dress to my underslip.

Dirndl skirts gave way to the shapeless sack; duffle coats and school scarves yielded to huge baggy hand-knitted black wool sweaters worn over trousers. We tapered the legs so much that we had to lie on the floor to wriggle into them. Having contemptuously cast aside flat shoes in favour of grown-up winklepickers on which we teetered around the town, we now slopped nonchalantly about in squashy flatties.

Tight skirts and button up cardigans worn back to front would, we hoped, emphasise our budding figures. The less well-endowed of us wore stiff padded bras. At the end of a smoochy number by Frank Sinatra or Connie Francis, when we'd been happily pressed against the chest of our partner, we'd glance down quickly, before moving apart, to check furtively whether the bra cones, far from filled, had become inverted.

After Brigitte Bardot's first film hit a stunned Lincoln, we all tried to assume a sensual pout. With our collection of plastic Indian bangles running from wrist to elbow, our wine-label patterned skirts, chestnut hair rinses which had a nasty habit of turning orange when inexpertly applied, we felt we'd reached the height of glamour.

We were momentarily stopped in our tracks when Simone Signoret appeared in the film of John Braine's novel *Room At The Top*. To our chagrin, it seemed that every hot-blooded male in the country envied Joe Lampton's seduction, not of the wealthy mill-owner's virginal daughter Susan, but the sophisticated middle-aged Frenchwoman. 'But she's old enough to be my mother!' I exclaimed. '*Grandmother*', muttered a schoolfriend. We were still too young and gauche.

Eager to increase our sophistication rating, we visited Boots cosmetic department and bought false eyelashes and false fingernails, blissfully unaware that if we were to wear them at the same time we'd need an additional three hours to get ready before going out in the evening.

It took me a couple of ham-fisted hours the first time to stick on my false nails, trying in a panic to remove the glue which had looped between my knuckles. The instructions warned that the adhesive was strong enough to stick aircraft carriers together and I feared turning my hands into mittens.

After the nails were painted a lurid silver-green, which took another half hour to dry, I set off, late, for my date. I was horror struck to discover on arrival at the boyfriend's home for supper that we, and other guests, were to play cards. Instead of spending the evening as I had fantasised, languidly gesturing to draw attention to my elegant hands, I found myself clawing desperately at the table top in an unsuccessful attempt to scoop up the cards, like a demented witch in a horror movie.

I went to the Camp Stack, as the cinema was called on the base at RAF Scampton, with a friend whose father was an officer there. Our mistake. The film was Elvis Presley's *Jailhouse Rock*. How could a couple of teenage girls squeal uninhibitedly when surrounded by a hundred young airmen whistling and jeering at Elvis. 'They're just jealous,' we sneered. 'Spotty lot.'

As a member of the Lincoln Grammar Schools' Square Dance Group, I danced each week at South Park School. My parents paid for a course of ballroom dancing lessons at the Castle Ballroom but I was soon too busy throwing myself around with abandon to the sounds of Rock and Roll to bother with the waltz and the foxtrot. We jived in the Nettleham Village Institute and at the Ermine Youth Club and traipsed around Lincoln at weekends in a light-hearted group of friends. My companions were from the High School and embryonic young doctors, farmers, teachers and architects from the Lincoln and City Boys' Schools which were not co-educational in those days.

My parents had moved to a larger property on the other side of the High Street in Nettleham and there was space for an upstairs playroom where we all congregated. We painted the walls white then overlaid them with black handprints. We spent a messy afternoon putting black footprints across the ceiling. The room was furnished with the 'contemporary' furniture of the fifties: plastic woven oyster-shaped chairs, light wood coffee tables with black twisted metal legs and knobbly feet. A table tennis table added to the attraction. It soon began to wane when my father, a keen player, would insist on beating my friends.

We played an LP by Tom Lehrer, the master of black humour, over and over again, until we'd managed to take down all the lyrics. We stuck them up on big sheets of paper around the walls, suitably illustrated. My mother read the suggestive words to the Boy Scouts' marching song 'Be Prepared' and firmly suggested that I remove them.

The Dansette record player was never turned off: *Blueberry Hill;* Conway Twitty's *Only Make Believe;* Paul Anka's *Diana.* When Buddy Holly was tragically killed in a plane crash early in 1959, we sat in stunned silence, playing only his records for the entire evening; the best way we felt we could mourn him.

The gang met on Saturday afternoons for coffee at Stokes' on High Bridge in Lincoln. Saturday evenings we all went to a dance or to the cinema: The Regal, Grand, Savoy, or Ritz to see the latest 'Carry On' film with Kenneth Williams and Hattie Jacques. The girls swooned at Harvey Kruger, and our latest idol, John Saxon, in *These Wonderful Years.* At a time when teenagers lived at home until they married and few young men could afford their own cars, what was on screen was something of a backdrop to what was going on in the auditorium of a Saturday evening. The darkness, plush seats and absence of family, provided the perfect opportunity for entwining hands and arms and much experimental snogging. Much of the time was spent with eyes closed or faces pointing in any direction other than the screen. The films would momentarily capture the audience's attention when a frightening scene offered the excuse to cuddle up even closer, or bury a face in a warm neck.

But in those days it was all unpressured, light-hearted and affectionate. Boyfriends were friends not lovers; six or eight of us, in couples, sharing a row in a kind of communal privacy. It was only when two of our number paired off and went somewhere on their own that we realised their relationship might perhaps be somewhat more serious than ours.

After the film we headed for one of the coffee bars, particularly the incongruously named *The Petite Hamburger.* In the fifties many took on a tattily exotic Mediterranean air, with fishermen's nets draped across rough cast walls, orange bulbs in lamps made from chianti bottles and badly painted, lurid views of Capri and Sorrento tacked up behind the tables. When the '96' coffee bar

63.

25a. The '96' coffee bar. It is the white building on the right side of the picture

25b. Exterior of the coffee bar

25c. An interior view of the '96' coffee bar

was opened by Joy and Don Comber on Newland, with its minimalist decor, atmosphere of laid-back sophistication, and hissing cappuccino machine, we couldn't believe our luck.

The stretch of road where we parked outside the '96' had a steep camber. Slamming the door too hard one evening on a much-loved vintage Morris Cowley with a dickey seat, belonging to what quickly became an ex-boyfriend, I saw the entire yellowing side window crack. Geoffrey, the owner of the car, on happier evenings sang and played the guitar. I still can't hear one of his favourite songs, 'I'm Nobody's Child', without remembering my horror and guilt as the crack spread across the window.

We all travelled around in a collection of rattling old bone-shakers – MG's, Fords, and Austins – the doors often held on by string. We shivered on grass verges as yet another puncture was mended near the Pyewipe Inn, or flashed our lights urgently at other vehicles in our convoy when the unreliable petrol gauge hadn't given due warning that we were about to run out.

Roger Butters had an Austin Seven with an old kitchen tap on the bonnet as a mascot, curtains in the windows, and a sign in the back saying, 'Don't laugh, Madam, your daughter might be inside.'

After saying goodnight to a boyfriend who'd brought me home, I'd wait at the door willing the coughing and spluttering engine to start, wondering whether it would make it back to Lincoln.

One evening, having had a row with my escort, I stormed in and went straight to bed. I lay awake listening to the pathetic 'chunkatichunk' as the engine turned over and over but refused to fire, thinking with grim satisfaction that Someone was going to spend the night in his draughty car in Nettleham High Street. He didn't, for my father, with his usual tolerance, went out to help. I fell asleep while they were still tinkering with the engine.

At an age when I and my schoolfriends had discovered, however innocently, that there were definitely two sexes and we were delighted that it was so, we tended to dismiss, with the arrogance of youth, the thought that our mistresses at Christ's Hospital Girls' High School might have interesting and satisfying private lives.

We saw them as archetypal spinsters who filled their free time embroidering chair covers, collecting wild flower specimens or reading Learned Journals. We felt, along with Anon, that:

> 'Miss Buss and Miss Beale,
> Cupid's darts do not feel;
> How different from us,
> Are Miss Beale and Miss Buss.'

When a couple of men joined the formerly all-female staff and we saw mistresses giddily *flirting* with them, or out of school hours we accidentally bumped into a blushing mistress in the company of a man, we were pruriently astonished. Dismissing such men as 'at least forty' and obviously 'past it' we realised that, for some perverse reason, we *wanted* them to be different from us.

66.

10.

A ROUND THE TIME the Aldermaston marchers were warning us that our civilisation would end unless we 'Banned the Bomb' and politically aware Youth became concerned about the future, Nettleham was consumed with curiosity at uncovering proof of its illustrious past. Archaeologists arrived in the village park by the Methodist chapel.

Nettleham Manor, more frequently referred to as The Bishop's Palace, had been a large country house built around the time of the Battle of Hastings in 1066. King Henry I granted it to the Bishop of Lincoln in 1101. On 25th January 1301, King Edward I arrived in Nettleham as Bishop d'Alderby's guest. Shortly afterwards, on the 7th February, the king created his eldest son: Earl of Carnarvon, Prince of Wales and Earl of Chester at Nettleham Manor.

The house and its dependencies must have been extensive, for the king brought with him over 600 horsemen, and both animals and men would have required food and accommodation. The house had a fine banqueting hall, some 44 feet long and 15 feet broad. There were gardens and a chapel to the west; a farmstead and stables to the east. The property was protected by walls, ditches and on one side what was then known as the Great Beck, and which today is a stream flowing through the village over-populated by garrulous ducks.

Little more was heard of the property until 1536 when it was vandalised in the Louth uprising although it remained in use for another fifty years. By 1630 the property was in such a dangerous state that a recommendation was made that it be demolished.

My sister and I had long heard rumours about a secret underground passage which ran between the Manor House and Lincoln Cathedral. We had spent happy times over the years wandering around the park tentatively prodding the ground with our toes, hoping that a yawning cavern would suddenly open up beneath our feet revealing the passage. This would ensure our reputation as intrepid explorers and we'd become as well-known as Enid Blyton's *Famous Five*. Now we eagerly awaited the results of the excavation.

The archeologists uncovered a well and found wood and some pottery urns. They dug up some fragments of Roman pottery (which suggested the site lay close to a Roman settlement) and others from Saxo-Norman, Middle-Saxon and Medieval periods. All this was very anti-climactic and bitterly disappointing to us. We felt that if the archaeologists couldn't unearth the passage at least they could have come up with some gruesome skeletons, jewellery, or Excalibur-like swords.

Towards the end of the fifties, the pattern of entertainment in Lincoln began to change. Pop stars and groups packed the ABC Savoy for one-night stands: Marty Wilde; The Bachelors and the Viscounts; Cliff Richard and the Drifters. (Tickets were 6/6d in the stalls.)

When Red Logan and his jazz band started the Lincoln Jazz Club in the loft above Dr. Blakelock's garages in Clarke's Yard on the Brayford in 1959 we were ecstatic. Using our favourite expressions of the time: Lincoln was suddenly 'blissful'. The Jazz Club was 'diggish'. We jived 'real solid'.

The club became so popular that there were fears that the floorboards wouldn't be able to support our weight and the Lincolnshire Echo would be provided with the dramatic headline: LINCOLN'S YOUTH IN DEATH PLUNGE. The club moved to the claustrophobic hut behind the Crowne pub on Clasketgate.

One night a week we forgot about Rock and Roll and gave

26. *Jazz Club membership card, 2/6d half-yearly subscription. Dated inside 18th March 1959*

68.

ourselves up to foot-stomping traditional jazz. There were visiting bands, including the South Bank Jazz Band from Grimsby, and specials such as Chris Barber. At Christmas the Jazz Club Fancy Dress Ball was held in the Assembly Rooms. Passers-by were startled to see the arrival of the Klu Klux Klan, half a dozen St. Trinian's look-a-likes, Pocahontas, the odd wizard, and a Roman nervously clutching his slipping toga.

Elaine Smith won first prize as a hula girl in what was certainly an inflammatory if not inflammable grass skirt. I won second prize as an Apache dancer: black split skirt, navy and white horizontally striped sweater, black stockings and French beret.

George Melly, who was playing with the Cy Laurie Jazz Band that night, asked me for my blue garter in which I'd stuck a plastic dagger. I watched proudly as he added it to his already extensive collection hanging from his double bass. It wasn't until the next day when my euphoria had evaporated that I remembered I had borrowed the garter and that it would now be on its way to Nottingham or Leeds.

John Roberts, who for many years has had an internationally renowned architectural practice in Lincoln, was then in the early days of his career. Even at that time, however, he could be relied upon to bring some much needed spice to the city. He gave a party to which I was taken by one of his young trainee architects. Somewhat overwhelmed by the seeming sophistication of the occasion, I drank a couple of glasses of what proved to be a lethal gin-based punch and found myself virtually legless. I turned to see a gentleman standing beside me. Memory insists, although this might be an indication of the fuddled state of my brain at the time, that he was wearing a bowler hat. 'And what do *you* do?' I asked, haughtily. 'I'm John Roberts,' he replied.

My escort, overcome with embarrassement at my inability to recognise The Great Man Himself, beat a hasty retreat with me in shameful tow. He had an ancient Riley with a gap in the floorboards on the passenger side. I supposed it served me right that on this particular evening it had been raining. I arrived home not only with the proverbial egg all over my face, but with Lincolnshire mud splashed all over my legs. The following morning, suffering my first hangover, I felt that perhaps he'd over-reacted. He was much too 'square'. Marlon Brando, I decided, would have handled it all with much greater aplomb.

Brought up in a family where books were as vital to life as breathing, from an early age I had harboured a secret desire to be a writer.

At the age of ten I scrawled my first, unfinished novel, all twenty-five pages of it; the chapter headings writ large and underlined in red. I bombarded people with letters. My father would come home to find me gloating over yet another pile of untouched paper which I was about to deface and remind me that forests in Finland were being chopped down daily just to keep me supplied.

We all read in the bath, waiting for the milk to boil over, on buses, in cars, while mixing Yorkshire puddings or washing up with spattered volumes wedged behind the kitchen taps. Naturally in bed and habitually at table.

Not that this interfered with conversation. We'd discuss the events of our day and then, at some ungiven but mutually accepted signal, it would be out with the books and down with the eyes. Concentration was fierce. If the Flying Scotsman had hurtled through the dining-room, hands would have been raised absent-mindedly and Lincolnshire pikelets thrown at its departing carriages without so much as a glance.

And woe betide anyone present who broke the library rule of Silence. Once, temporarily without reading matter and feeling neglected, surrounded by bent heads, I held what I thought was an amusing conversation with myself. No-one found it in the last bit amusing or took pity on my isolation. I was told, very firmly, to shut up.

Well aware that reading at table was socially unacceptable, my mother insisted that books were banned when guests were present. This did not stop my sister, Jill, from being caught on a number of occasions with her head inclined at a somewhat painful angle, her hands making furtive darts beneath the corner of the tablecloth.

When I reached my teens I was eager to spread my still stickily-opening wings and didn't relish the thought of swotting subjects in which I had only a secondary interest in the hope of passing sufficient A-levels to gain a university place. I announced that I did not wish to try.

My decision to opt out didn't include a desire to rebel against my family. Neither my mother nor my father ever pressured me into anything. Having been witness to the pitiful pre-examination nerves of a schoolfriend whose father constantly pressured her, to the point of threats, to succeed, I was very grateful to mine. My father gave advice when consulted but invariably ended with: 'It's your life. I don't mind if you empty dustbins if you are convinced it will make you happy.' It was a philosophy of which my teachers would have wholeheartedly disapproved. Or so I thought.

It would have beeen understandable and justified if the High School mistresses had accused me of laziness. But, to my eternal gratitude, they were supportive. In the sixth form I spent long and satisfying periods in the library: reading, writing essays, studying current affairs, cataloguing books. I talked at length with Miss Bows, one of the mistresses, who subsequently came to live in Nettleham. She encouraged my creativity and gave ungrudgingly of her time; as did the delightful and eminently sane Mrs Reeves.

It was an ironic twist that some six years after I left a school at which it was felt I had never fulfilled my potential, I was invited back to address the assembled girls on Commemoration Day. News of my involvement by then in the theatre, of working on BBC television documentaries and with a controversial behavioural psychologist, had reached the ears of the careers mistress.

As I stood on the platform, smelling the suddenly familiar mixture of polish, ink, and chalk, I realised what a splendid education I had been given. I was determined that the school should be proud of me. I was also determined that my sister, now a pupil at the school but hiding in the cloakroom, too concerned for my sake to risk inhibiting me with her presence in the audience, should also be proud of me.

11.

I LEFT THE HIGH SCHOOL in July 1960 with mixed feelings compounded of sadness that a period of my life was over, relief that it was, and yet with a stomach-churning awareness that it was now my own responsibility to prepare myself for a stimulating and, I hoped, profitable future. I quickly enrolled in a private secretarial school near the racecourse in Lincoln.

It was run from her home by Miss Ellis, a sort of Miss Marple character, whose seemingly genteel exterior masked a steely determination that her small group of Young Ladies should be a credit to Mr. Pitman. I wasn't; soon finding that, however hard I tried to master the shorthand symbols, I could still scribble my own abbreviations faster. Typing I enjoyed enormously as I discovered the delight of producing words at a speed which, unlike using pen and ink, could keep up with my thoughts.

To increase our typing speeds we practised in the small old-fashioned front parlour to music on a wind-up gramophone. No sooner had we built up sufficient speed to tap in time with the music, than His Master's Voice gradually ran down, our speed instinctively slowing down with it, until the machine was furiously cranked up again and we raced to catch up. It was a difficult lesson to take seriously. Within a few months I had passed my shorthand and bookkeeping examinations with good grades and my typing examination with an excellent one. I subsequently increased my speed even further and in the years before the advent of the word-processor basked in the glory of having a typing speed which was only a couple of words a minute below the world record. As with all boasting this was a mixed blessing for, until I became self-employed, it simply meant I did twice the work but received the same salary as anyone else.

On my 17th birthday, the proud holder of a provisional driving licence, I drove the family to Skegness and back with an equally proud father sitting beside me. Before I was legally allowed onto the roads, my father wanted me to be comfortable with the car so he taught me to drive on a disused aerodrome close to Nettleham. We spent many happy hours together as I practised three-point turns, parking between stones laid on the runway, and wove in and out of obstacles. I also learned how to change a fan belt and identify all the bits and pieces under the bonnet.

Russia was still an enemy in those days and the airfield perimeter bristled with missiles. One evening, accidentally getting too close, we were startled to see an RAF fire engine bearing down on us, its occupants warning us to move away from the security area. We tactfully didn't tell them of the theory popular in Nettleham at the time that, if there had been a four-minute warning, their missiles would have created an international incident rather than devastation in Russia as they were believed to be pointing in the wrong direction.

As my parents refused to consider my leaving home at seventeen, and I couldn't legally please myself until I was twenty-one, I decided that sighing self-pityingly for four years would be as tedious for me as it was for them and looked for a job locally.

I joined an insurance office to brush up my shorthand and typing speeds and to gain some business experience. In the event I learned a great deal more than that. I wasn't so much liked as barely tolerated by the other girls in the typing pool on the top floor who were suspicious of anyone or anything which didn't conform to their norm.

They kept handkerchiefs stuffed up their cardigan sleeves; religiously observed birthdays with pneumatic over-stuffed cream cakes; brought out powder puffs, lipsticks and combs at exactly five minutes to five; covered their typewriters at two minutes to five and were out of the building as the clock struck the hour. The worlds of work and leisure were strictly divided.

I was given one of the first typewriters ever manufactured; long overdue for a museum. A small, ugly, sit-up-and-beg hunk of metal, it weighed half a ton. Its button-like keys were stiff and unwieldly and, unless hit with deadly accuracy, they jammed together against the paper in a fierce cluster which had to be disentangled slowly. It was impossible to produce clean, neat letters quickly. Nervous of wasting paper, I was forced to type ever more slowly only to find, to my intense frustration and embarrassment, that too often on the final word, perhaps having relaxed slightly at nearing the end of the letter, that the keys would jam and smudge the type. I could feel Miss Ellis from the Secretarial College tut-tutting over my shoulder.

Conscious that my work was not doing either of us justice, I knocked on the branch manager's door on the third day and asked if I might have another machine. Unaware that the pre-Boer War Imperial existed – branch managers, in those days, rarely visiting the typing pool – he apologised and arranged for a newer model to be on my desk the following morning.

I thought the girls would be delighted that at long last the offending object, the cause of such unnecessary labour, had been removed. But they were horrified by my behaviour. There was a stony silence for the remainder of the day. I was sent to Coventry. As soon as I left the room to take dictation the whispering started, and stopped the second I returned.

Too late, I realised my mistake. The typewriter was a primitive initiation ceremony which the junior was expected to endure: break her nails, bash her knuckles, and break her in. The age and size of each individual typewriter was an indication of the seniority of its operator and importance of her position – the quality of the work was secondary.

Never having worked in an office before, I now had to learn painfully the unspoken rules which operated in a typing pool: the sensitivity to hierarchy; the deferring to the senior girls; and the strict demarcation lines between a secretary and a shorthand typist.

The girls were responsible for making the tea and coffee each day and taking it up and around four floors by way of a very steep staircase from the basement kitchen. The steps were covered in shiny, worn linoleum; the tray, when filled with heavy white crockery and hot liquids, was dangerously heavy. It seemed ridiculous to me that in a building which contained a number of strong and good-natured young men, that the girls should carry the trays each day. Having learned my lesson, however, from The Trouble Over the Typewriter, I thought it wiser to keep my feelings to myself.

A combination of weak wrists and subconscious unwillingness on my part saved me the bother. One morning, I managed to stagger up the first two flights but at the corner of the second landing I slipped on the linoleum under the weight of the tray and, unable to save myself, fell backwards down the stairs followed by twenty cups and saucers, two jugs of milk, half a pound of granulated sugar, and two enormous pots of coffee; all in full view of the insurance clerks working in the open plan ground floor area.

The crashing brought everyone out onto the landings. The sight of smashed crockery and rivulets of liquid pouring over my prostrate body, teaspoons hopping and clattering down a step at a time, must have been agreeably dramatic. I was taken home, somewhat shaken, with a tea towel wrapped around a scalded arm.

The boys took it in turns to carry the trays after that – willingly – but the girls never forgot it nor forgave me, seeing it as an insult and a shameful admission of weakness by US in front of THEM.

The girls, I am sure, were never knowingly unkind to me nor realised how nervous they made me but I was made abundantly aware that our attitudes were so diametrically opposed that there could never be more than an uneasy peace however much I might try to placate. I stuck it out for as long as I could but around the time Yuri Gagarin was shot into space I felt that, although I didn't want to change places with him, my life certainly lacked excitement by comparison and it was time I lifted off from the world of insurance.

One evening, some weeks later, when conversation had been given its allotted time, my family were all reading at table as usual. My father was hidden behind a searing exposé of 'The Men Who Control America'. My mother, smiling dreamily, was lost in the sunlit world of Dornford Yates; of fast cars and the soft plop of tennis balls on country house courts. My sister, academically the brightest of the lot of us, was engrossed in the poetry of Gerard Manley Hopkins, her lips moving as she silently relished the music of his words. I, too, wanted to be transported from my humdrum existence, but eager to find something closer to home was scanning, without much hope of success, The Lincolnshire Echo.

The headlines screamed the important news of the day: Town Council Agrees to New Zebra Crossing. There were the usual photographs of principal guests at a Round Table dinner and bemused foreigners inspecting the mayorial Chains of Office over cups of Nescafe. Three motorists had been fined for minor offences and, as was often the case, one of the culprits was an RAF Cranwell cadet. The small ads, with ambiguous brevity, offered: Size 40 wedding dress & two pink bridesmaids, £6 the lot.

I turned to the jobs section: Chicken Sexers Wanted; Tractor Driver; Part-time Lady for Steep Hill Corsets. I sighed. There didn't seem to be anything there likely to blast me into an exciting new world of discovery but then, even Yuri Gagarin had had to return to earth. Then I saw it: **Secretary Required for Lincoln Repertory Theatre Company.**

I let out a piercing whistle to express my delighted astonishment and in an attempt to attract the attention of my family. No-one even bothered to look up. 'Lincoln Theatre is advertising for a secretary,' I said, very loudly.

'I don't think so, darling,' said mother. My mother had and still has an oblique way of replying. I knew she didn't mean the theatre *wasn't* advertising; simply that I wasn't going to be allowed to apply for the position. Although Mother had been a keen amateur theatre producer for many years, nevertheless she had a distaste for unconventional behaviour, blissfully unaware that she was fundamentally unconventional herself. The tone in which her words had been uttered held a shorthand peculiar to Mother. It implied the *professional* theatre was a centre for orgies; it might be magical when viewed from the audience's side of the proscenium arch, but if I thought I was going to cross over the footlights and join the Bohemians I had another serious think coming.

'When?' asked my sister.

'Immediately,' I replied, dashing my hopes. I was going to Italy for a holiday. Even if I could persuade my mother to change her mind, no-one would wait three weeks for me. And anyway, by now the applicants would be queuing up outside the theatre with their bedrolls and primus stoves. Interesting jobs appeared in Lincoln with the same regularity as little green men in flying saucers – or rather, in those days, little Russian men in space ships.

I decided to apply anyway. I was accepted. Babs Robinson, the secretary at the time, agreed to stay on until I returned from my Italian holiday. I liked her immediately. After a family pow-wow my mother had relented although I was firmly told that I could only work with theatricals on the understanding that I didn't get *involved*, which was a bit like telling an opera singer that she could walk on to the stage at Covent Garden but must not open her mouth. Coming from my mother, this was very funny. In our family whatever we did we got involved – mother most of all.

Who had encouraged me to tread the boards all those years ago, I reminded her. Who had given me and my sister our love of words? Who had recently raved about a Lincoln Theatre production of *The Boyfriend*?

'Oh do shut up,' said Mother, with some justification.

27. *Lincoln Repertory Theatre Company – The Boyfriend*

12.

SUNTANNED AND BURSTING WITH MEMORIES of shooting stars over Capri, liquid-eyed Italian boys, and running at dawn with Patty Phillips around the deserted Olympic athletic track in Rome, acknowledging the cheers of invisible crowds, I returned to Nettleham. I had begun what would be a life-long love affair with Italy but was now eager to begin my new job at the theatre or rather, cliché as it may be, to breathe a new life

The theatre *did* have a unique aroma, compounded of the greasepaint in the dressing rooms; the acrid scent of size for stiffening scenery; the pervading damp fustiness in the gloomy, echoing passages; the fuggy combination of cigarette smoke, duplicating ink and dust in the tiny office which I shared with the front of house manager, Harry Whitfield, and Babs Robinson, who now came in two days a week.

Babs, petite, vivacious with fine-boned Gallic features, was the ideal companion. Nothing was ever too much trouble for her; everything was interesting, fun, worth doing well. A natural hard worker, she did everything perfectly herself but was quite convinced others could do it better, We shared confidences, cigarettes, coped with the company crises, ducked when Kay Gardner, the manager, a handsome, imposing woman, had one of her steaming tantrums, and enjoyed every second of it all.

Our office was cluttered but cosy; Babs and I facing one another at ancient scratched desks which snagged nylon stockings at least once a day. We perched beside the window in a part of the room which stuck out over the cobbled courtyard at the side like a grand tier box. An old safe in the corner held we knew not what, never having been opened in living memory. Shelves, overlaid with dust, housed files and old scripts; the dirty nicotine stained walls, undecorated for twenty years, were covered in posters of past productions.

The rattle of pails each morning signalled the arrival of the perennially cheerful Olive and her merry band of sardonic cleaners who marched into the auditorium, fags stuck between their lips, to do battle with the mess left by the previous night's audience. The bangings and clatterings were accompanied by succinct comments about the disgusting places people chose to stick their flaming ice-cream wrappers or chewing gum. Olive would appear in the office with a long-suffering expression on her face, holding up a glove, a spectacle case, a diary or a scarf: 'Thank Gawd their 'eds aren't loose.'

Tepid weak coffee in chipped mugs arrived at eleven when the company broke rehearsal and headed for the peeling green room. We stayed front of house, bashing away on old manual typewriters, trotting between our office and the front office overlooking Clasketgate shared by the manager, Kay Gardner, and the theatre director, Kenneth V. Moore, known as 'K.V.'

There was an enormous cupboard just to the left of their door which housed the memorabilia of the theatre: faded curling photographs of glamorous actresses and handsome actors – most of them unknown faces who, from the dates stamped on the back, were probably now married, leading respectable lives, working perhaps in an insurance office. Occasionally, with a shock of recognition, a face of someone who had made it: a poignantly youthful version of an actor or actress whose present more mature photograph was pasted up outside a West End theatre; the target of adoring fans waiting eagerly outside the stage door for autographs.

There were catalogues, old ballet shoes, cracked tap dancing pumps, playbooks, pathetic letters pleading for jobs, old audition lists with the director's comments scrawled beside the names: *Too old. Not enough sparkle. She's no ingenue! Terrible legs. Possible. Perhaps Panto,* or just plain *No! No! No!*

A whole new language had to be learned: the names of drama schools: Rose Bruford, Webber Douglas, RADA and LAMDA; Monty Berman, the theatrical costumiers; Strand Electric and lighting equipment – brutes and spots and floods. *Spotlight* was the director's 'casting bible' – heavy volumes containing photographs and listing previous roles of virtually every actor and actress in the country. The famous could afford a full page; the aspiring unknowns sharing a page with three or more others. I learned to be wary of the glossy, beautifully lit and flattering portraits, particularly those by Michael Barrington Studios in which every actress, long-lashed and high-cheekboned, had the glamour of a Hollywood star. When newcomers arrived to join the company for a couple of productions, I was shocked and, I suppose, relieved to discover just how ordinary they looked until, in stage make-up they appeared on stage and the magic transformation took place again.

There was office work like no other. Letters to the Arts Council and Local Authorities pleading for money, money, money, grants, grants, grants, caused much agonising over their composition: making clear the urgency of our need, demonstrating the value of the contribution we were making to the cultural well-being of Lincolnshire, but without *grovelling*. We lived under a constant siege of bills and Final Notices with the threat of closure hanging over our heads like the sword of Damocles. Harry Whitfield took the brunt of this.

Harry, the front of house manager, was a tall, stooping, spare figure, balding, bespectacled, exuding sanity. He and his beloved wife, Phil, had been licensees of the The Bowling Green public house in Lincoln for many years before his retirement – at which time he came to work at the theatre. He never lost his temper; coped kindly with the constant pleas for subs from petty cash which broke out like an epidemic a couple of days before pay day; dealt with irate creditors; organised the box office staff, usherettes and barmen, and attempted to keep the books in order in a business where holding a financial head above water required someone capable of walking on it. Harry was a perfect foil for the frequent creative excesses of backstage and much loved by all of us.

We typed scripts, organised auditions and found digs for visiting actors in what was the traditional theatrical digs area around Spring Hill. When occasionally stumped for accommodation, we arranged for them to be put up for a night in one of the police cells in the Sessions House at the bottom of Lindum Hill. Thanks to the agreement of goodhearted policemen who were keen theatregoers and the fact that Lincoln's criminal element in those days was small, there was usually a vacant cell. 'Actually,' said one appreciative actor, 'it was really rather cosy in the clink. I was woken up with a lovely hot cup of tea in the morning.'

We filled in Performing Rights Society sheets (royalties had to be paid to composers for any of their music used during a performance). We prepared the programme material each week for the long-suffering, kindly Mr. Melton; a Pickwickian figure of a printer full of good humour and astonishing patience when it came to getting his bills paid. The distinctive red and white posters and playbills for forthcoming productions were distributed throughout Lincoln. Although the theatre had its own wardrobe, for special Shakespearian and costume drama productions, the richly trimmed, historically authentic costumes were ordered from Monty Berman. These arrived in huge wicker skips like magical dressing-up boxes for grown-ups.

Furnishing the sets for a weekly succession of plays required a constantly changing series of props: furniture, ornaments, pictures, which were begged or borrowed from a number of local shopkeepers and theatregoers who were generous in their willingness to loan items to us.

The then Dean of Lincoln, The Rt. Rev. Colin Dunlop and his wife were enthusiastic and loyal supporters. In one production, the actor Ronald Herdman had to appear on stage in a pair of old-fashioned striped pyjamas. The stage manager thought he knew just the person who might still be wearing them. He knocked on the Deanery door and spoke to Mrs. Dunlop. A package changed hands. On the opening night the Dean and his wife were sitting front stalls and on came Ronald. The Dean turned to his wife. 'He's wearing pyjamas just like mine, dear,' he said. 'They *are* yours,' replied his wife in an equally loud whisper.

Within weeks of my arrival at the theatre my own family's personal possessions and furniture started to disappear and then reappear not necessarily in the same state or colour in which they had originally left. A wicker chair was needed for *A Passage to India.* I telephoned my father and told him, in somewhat garbled fashion, that we were doing an Indian production and that someone would be collecting the chair. Later that morning there was a knock on the kitchen door. Father opened it to find a turbanned Indian on the doorstep. Before he could open his mouth, father shook him cheerfully by the hand and said: 'Do come in. It's in the first room on the left at the top of the stairs.' The brush salesman fled. An hour later, the stage manager arrived and took the chair away brown. It went back yellow.

There was a marked difference between front of house and backstage – two distinct areas, the boundary marked by a groaning, steel fire door. The long corridors were full of eery shadowswhere the ghost of Hamlet lurked, and distant echoes of decades of declamation.

The auditorium was familiar. As a child I'd been a regular theatregoer and felt at home there: the red plush seats; the horseshoe circle; the stone-stepped Gods where, at one performance, a young mother engrossed in the play, had forgotten her baby sleeping on her lap. It had rolled down to the front where, rudely woken by its painful, bumpy progress, it had howled loudly and lengthily, temporarily stopping the performance. The heavy red curtain which separated the actors from the audience had always induced a curled knot of anticipation and expectation as it rose at the beginning of a play.

Now it was different, the curtain was up during the day. A new world was open to me in all its nakedness. Actors stood in the middle of the stage scratching heads, chatting, arguing, pacing out moves, reading lines aloud, staring into space, trying not to show disappointment at casting sessions when the hoped for leading part did not materialise. Scene painters yelled at the actors to 'Get out of the way PERLEESE', as they charged across carrying steaming evil-smelling buckets of size. Stage flats, so artfully lit during performances, lay drunkenly against the back wall with half a garden obliterated by a newly painted castle turret being overlaid for the next production. The world of theatre is a world of illusion, delusion and sadly often disallusion; but the prospect of fame is a potent driving force.

The lighting board, so ancient it looked as if it had been cobbled together in a moment of madness by a demented Professor wearing opaque bi-focals, was a short circuit to oblivion. The wood in the sets, the rickety, perilously narrow gantry way up in the flies attracting an updraft, the dust and paint, provided potential fire hazards.

However often the management comforted themselves with the statistics which showed English theatres to be among the safest in the world, they lived in morbid dread of the Fire Inspector. The news that inspection time had come round again reduced them to a state of gibbering terror followed by a demoniac hoovering of the grid and a frantic clear-out. On one occasion, the manager, seeing for the first time a gloriously paper-flower-bedecked set designed by Rosemary Jaynes, fell back in a state of apoplexy screaming: 'Are you absolutely, positively certain that those flaming flowers are fire proof?'

If a fire were to break out in the theatre, the password for the company and staff was the playing of a scratched and tinny 78 recording of 'The Teddy Bears' Picnic': on hearing the music we were all, supposedly, to move into our fire-drill which we practised from time to time. We learned that they did things (with much greater panache) in Australia.

Douglas Milvain, a member of the Lincoln Theatre Company and Australian by birth, had briefly worked as a cinema manager in Australia in the early days of his acting career. If a fire started in the cinema Douglas was in-structed to appear on stage before the cinema screen and, pointing a loaded revolver at the audience, shout: 'I'll shoot the first person who panics!' Dougie naturally fantasised about how he would deliver this dramatic gift of a line to an actor and whether, in the event, he'd actually be able to bring himself to pull the trigger. Happily both for Dougie and the Australian cinema audience, the occasion never arose. But it seems likely that the shock of such a threat would have removed, as was its admirable intention, the necessity to do so.

28. *Lincoln Repertory Theatre 1961*

29. *The Merchant of Venice*
(with Audrey Barr – a Lincolnian – as Portia)

84.

13.

SHORTLY BEFORE I JOINED the theatre in September 1961, the director, Kenneth ('K.V.') Moore, curious to learn what the people of Lincoln thought about their theatre and keen to encourage a wider audience, sent members of the company out onto the streets and into the engineering works to conduct a survey. He was chastened by the discovery that many of the city's residents didn't even know that the theatre existed.

Today, those same Lincoln residents would be equally chastened to learn just how many of the young and talented actors and actresses who stopped to talk to them in the street and who could be seen weekly on the stage of the Theatre Royal, subsequently became well-known in television, films and the West End. Stephanie Cole *(Waiting for God)*; Brigit Forsyth *(The Likely Lads)*; Philip Madoc, Freddie Jones, Gerald Blake, Roger Redfarn, and Penelope Keith.

James Loughran was engaged as musical director for *The Boyfriend.* He took a few hours off one day to enter the Philharmonia Orchestra's conducting competition; returning to Lincoln Theatre to play the piano for that evening's performance. Winning first prize in the competition launched his distinguished career which has included conducting the BBC Symphony Orchestra, major orchestras around the world and the Proms. From 1971-83 he was principal conductor of the Hallé.

Michael Billington, writer and drama critic for The Guardian, The Times, New York Times and Illustrated London news, and IPC's Critic of the Year in 1974, was Public Liaison Officer at the Theatre Royal from 1962-4.

K.V. Moore was a talented director who, in the spring of 1961 had been awarded an Arts Council Travel Fellowship, enabling him to spend some weeks in turn with three of the most revered and influential European theatrical companies of the time: Bertold Brecht's Berliner Ensemble in East Berlin (with Helena Weigel); the

Comédie française in Paris; and Ingmar Bergman's group in Sweden. After his years at Lincoln he directed at the Mermaid Theatre and was Assistant Director of Olivier's *Othello* and Zefferelli's *Much Ado About Nothing.*

During my first week at the theatre, rehearsals were underway for *The French Mistress.* Bringing a cup of coffee into the auditorium for Kenneth, I stayed to watch for a few minutes. Brigit Forsyth, whose dark prettiness and youthful innocence made her an ideal juvenile lead, had been cast in the part of Lisette Latour. Penny Keith, whose height and more sophisticated good looks barred her from such young romantic leads, had been cast, yet again, in a character part – this time as Mrs. Barlow – which meant she would be made-up to look older than she was. Penny was having a good-natured moan about this.

'Penny,' said Kenneth, 'when you actually reach the age you so often portray on stage, you will be a huge star'. When *The Good Life* hit our television screens some years later, I realised just how astute Kenneth had been.

In no time at all I became involved – which didn't surprise my family – and spent as much time as I could at the theatre. The company couldn't help but be romantic to a seventeen-year old girl. Before the advent of the sixties Hippies, the theatre had its own bohemian look: the actresses' ethnic skirts, clanking jewellery and long stride; and the actors' corduroy jackets, battered cavalry twill trousers, cravats and long hair. Not to be outdone, I bought a fake leopard skin bowler hat and a long brown suede coat – which were greeted with less than enthusiasm by my family.

The company's seeming confidence and veneer of sophistication inhibited me at first, but gradually I saw beneath the bright smiles young men and women living on the financial edge the whole time (the top salary was less than £15 a week; I earned £6.10s.), wondering whether, when their contracts finished at Lincoln, there would be parts available elsewhere. There was no climbing up the ladder of promotion with the reward of a secure salary and a director's nameplate on the office door; but there was the seductive spur of having one's name up in lights at any age if

30. *The Hostage – Lincoln Repertory Theatre 25th July 1961*

the right part, right play or praise from the right critic catapulted an unknown to stardom.

Insecure, unsure of themselves but determined to succeed, it was understandable that strong bonds developed between them; that they moved in a separate and private world. Nothing brings people closer together than a shared love of theatre and nothing divides faster than the jealousy of being overshadowed, of talent not being given a chance to shine. A combination of youth, enthusiasm, and sheer hard work made Lincoln Theatre Company a happy one most of the time. It was inevitable that working in such close proximity six days and evenings a week there would be ructions but these were usually dissolved in laughter.

Jolyon H. Coombs, the stage manager for some months, managed, unwittingly, to annoy the somewhat artistically temperamental set designers when we were playing *The Eagle Has Two Heads*, an intense two-hander by Cocteau starring Roger Redfarn as Stanilas and Sheila Price as The Queen.

The final scene took place at the top of a grand staircase in a 'Ruritanian' palace. The staircase, thanks to the artifice of the set, looked imposingly solid. As the play built to its climax – the murder and suicide of the two protagonists – Sheila Price was sprawled dead on the stairs as Roger tumbled down equally dead beside her. Unfortunately, he fell with such force that the bannister slid away from the steps revealing the backstage wall of the theatre in all its rough-hewn tattiness. On it, someone had whitewashed in large letters: JOLYON H COOMBS MUST GO! Sheila and Roger, feigning dead in what should have been the final, poignantly dramatic moment of the play and expecting it to be met with suitably stunned silence, were bewildered to hear the curtain coming down on an audience doubled up with laughter.

However little The Man in the Street might have known about Lincoln's Theatre Royal, the company enjoyed the patronage of an enthusiastic and loyal group of supporters. The Lincoln Theatre Association had been formed in 1955 by the then director, John Hale, and a group of public-spirited individuals. By 1961 it had developed into a Theatre Partnership involving four towns within a fifty mile radius: Loughborough, Scunthorpe, and Rotherham, with Lincoln as the centre of the production circuit.

The chairman of the Association during my time at the theatre was Dr. Charles Lillicrap, for thirty years one of Lincoln's most prominent and respected citizens: consultant physician, mayor, chairman of the housing committee (where he made an important contribution to solving Lincoln's post-war housing problems), he wore his various hats with wit and distinction. It was largely thanks to his efforts that the theatre survived several difficulties in its early years. His good humour and commonsense contributed enormously.

He delighted in telling of his early days as a physician when, visiting farmers on some of the isolated Fenland farms, he found many of them sewn up by their wives for the winter in red flannel. When a couple of Indian junior doctors arrived at Lincoln and were having trouble learning English, Dr. Lillicrap suggested that in their free time they should watch television in the doctors' common room. Their English didn't seem to be improving, however, and one day as Dr. Lillicrap was passing the open door of the common room he understood why: coinciding with the pair's rest periods, the BBC was transmitting programmes in Welsh.

Alderman John Spence ('Jack') was chairman of the Theatre Club and he, his wife Nora and three sons shared a great love of live theatre. Mayor of Lincoln from 1969-70, he later became chairman of the Federation of Playgoers Societies. I was delighted to meet him frequently on First Nights in what were now very different circumstances; for he had been branch manager and thus my boss at the insurance company. When I gave in my notice he had been understandably more sympathetic than most bosses when he learned where I planned to work next.

Audiences liked the intimacy of a repertory system and were loath to see extensive changes in the company, preferring to watch the same faces whom they had come to know well, playing totally different parts each week and extending their range.

One of the company's most popular productions, and an ambitious departure from their usual work on stage, had been K.

V. Moore's innovative adaptation of Tennyson's *Idylls of the King*, presented as an open-air pageant in Riseholme Park. Sir Charles Tennyson, the poet's grandson, acted as text adviser.

It wasn't until the pageant had been announced and casting begun that Kenneth learned that with one notable exception – Douglas Milvain – members of the company either couldn't ride or had only ridden as children Thelwell-style; not very reassuring when two opposing armies on horseback were to meet and clash. Dougie was a fine horseman who had ridden in the Australian outback. He was, understandably, given the part of Sir Lancelot – who most certainly couldn't be seen to fall off his horse. Turning the other members of the company into an impressive troop of riders was out of the question, finances and time being what they were, so they had to make do with half a dozen lessons at the local riding school supplemented by reckless courage.

The pageant played to large and enthusiastic audiences. In one scene the opposing armies on horseback had to meet, fight and then retreat. The horses had come from the same stables and were, naturally, rather fond of one another. Sir Lancelot's mount, after the battle, decided to trot off merrily with his pals on the opposing side.

On the first night, the guests of honour were the Earl of Ancaster, Sir Charles Tennyson, the Bishop of Lincoln and Sir John Betjeman. Glancing briefly in their direction after the performance, Kenneth saw them strolling arm in arm, deep in conversation, none of them in the first flush of youth; blissfully unaware that they were heading for a thick guy rope securing one of the marquees. Before warning them in time, Kenneth had a split second, horrific vision of his illustrious guests tripping simultaneously over the rope and leaving the pageant side by side on stretchers.

The boat in which Queen Guinevere sailed on the lake was borrowed from the Lincoln Sea Scouts and sank in the excitement. The sword of Excalibur was attached to an ingenious pulley system operated by a lever hidden on the bank. At the moment when a spotlight lit the water, Excalibur rose from the depths

31. *K. V. Moore – left, with the Earl of Ancaster – centre (The Lord Lieutenant of Lincolnshire) and Sir Charles Tennyson*

accompanied by admiring oohs and ahs from the audience.

At the end of the pageant's run, mud and weeds had become so entangled with the lever mechanism that the sword could not be retrieved. When the cast finally departed, it was left behind. As far as I know, it is still there. I like to think that one moonlit night, the sword will rise from beneath the waters, and archaeologists cheerfully claim that the magic Excalibur *was* returned on King Arthur's death to the Lady of the Lake; that the story was not myth but reality; and that Riseholme Park must have been the true seat of King Arthur and his court.

Some months later, Sir Charles Tennyson was to join Kenneth and Kay Gardner for tea at the theatre. Kay had one of her famous tantrums about the chipped and stained theatre crockery. I brought in a tea set of Mother's: blue with white spots which she had bought some years before from Frank Gadsby's shop in Lincoln, and Sir Charles was given an elegantly served tea. A man of dignity and charm, still sporting a wing collar, it was obvious when we met that he wouldn't have been the least bit concerned about drinking from an old pot theatre mug.

The method of production at Lincoln was a complicated one made necessary by the touring partnership. Simply, it meant that two companies, each with actors, director, set designer and stage management staff, were fully employed simultaneously, working alternately one week in Lincoln and the next week on tour with a basic fortnight's rehearsal schedule. A play would open in Lincoln for a week with company A and then go to one of the three touring towns the next week; company B returning from their week in Loughborough, Scunthorpe or Rotherham to appear in the next production at Lincoln. It was a punishing schedule involving extremely hard work and long hours.

The companies rehearsed each morning and then, after lunch or a snack at Boots (which had a marvellous cafe upstairs in those days), the company which was touring that week left on the coach. They travelled in all weathers, sometimes not returning until well after midnight; in winter a prey to fog and ice.

Only once was the coach involved in an accident – when it hit a cow. John Ronane was on crutches for a time but continued to appear on stage. Each evening he hobbled to the wings and then, abandoning his crutches, sang and danced in Noel Coward's *Red Peppers* before limping off-stage to grab his crutches once more; a fine example of The Show Must Go On.

And it usually did – apart from the inevitable alarums which over the years have helped to swell the collective coffers of disaster stories beloved by the theatrical profession; – those 'Do you remember the night when . . .' reminiscences. Raymond Llewellyn, worn out after playing a large part on tour the previous week, fell asleep during a performance of *Anne Frank* and had to be nudged awake when his cue came.

In *Arsenic and Old Lace*, he accidentally caught an electric cable with his walking stick as he was about to make his entrance and inadvertently dragged it on stage with him whereupon, to cover this with 'business', he beat it to death in a frenzy.

The curtain once rose on a play and took part of the set up with it. Frederick Hall made his entrance through the fireplace.

The witches' cauldron in *Macbeth* caught fire.

14.

HE WEEKS BEFORE CHRISTMAS were charged with the kind of anticipation unique to the theatre: the build-up to the annual Christmas pantomime which opened on Boxing Day, when the auditorium would be filled with the sympathetic warmth of families and the uninhibited enjoyment, participation, and sometimes dauntingly vocal criticism, of children.

The pantomimes, all written by Kenneth Moore during his years at Lincoln, were old-fashioned, traditional family entertainments; no dirty jokes, no references to pop stars – just a be-rouged, ungainly Dame, an impossibly long-legged and glamorous Principal Boy, and as much visual magic as could be conjured up by our limited budget but richly talented scenic designers and carpenters whose practical work provided the framework for the fantasy.

One of the highlights each year was the UV (ultra-violet-lit) scenes: dance sequences performed by the superbly trained members of Christine Orange's Dancing School in Lincoln who were known affectionately by everyone in the theatre as 'The Pippins'. Three of the talented dancers – Hilary Sladden, John and Susan Toogood I had known from my school days and Sue had been on the Rome and Capri holiday with me. Christine Orange choreographed the pantomime numbers but, like everyone else in the theatre, often found herself dealing with more than she'd bargained for when last minute panics arose. One afternoon, when a matinee was about to start, she discovered that the costumes had been left at the laundrette. Christine rushed down to collect them only to find that they were still damp. She had no choice but to allow her dancers to wear them while she watched guiltily from the wings, praying no-one would catch a chill, as the costumes steamed during the energetic dance numbers.

Babs and I typed the pantomime script onto huge foolscap stencils then turned them off on our ancient, clanking, duplicating machine; up to our elbows in ink.

At the first reading of *Dick Whittington*, written by Kenneth, two of the Dame's malapropisms turned out to be typing errors, but as they got the loudest laughs from the cast at the read-through they stayed in. Bab's perceptive eyes spotted a couple of things which were meant to be in: the naming of Dick's cat *Sukie*, and the pirate ship: *The Saucy Sue*. 'I wonder' said Babs, looking pointedly at me, 'whether that was intentional.' It was, but it would be a couple of months before either of us realised fully what lay behind it.

Dick Whittington opened in the coldest weather for many years – snow, ice and temperatures below those of Moscow. As theatrical digs were heated by small electric or gas fires and the theatre notoriously draughty, the company was prey to coughs and colds. Penny Keith fell ill with influenza during the run and for a few days her parts as Queen Neptune and Queen Salome of Morocco were taken over by Gerry Blake in drag, not knowing a word.

Dick Whittington's cat was played by Gerry's wife, Sally Wyndham-Davies, in a tight-fitting and claustrophobic cat costume. She was some months pregnant at the time and there were fears that this pantomime cat might be the first one in theatrical history to produce kittens on stage. In the event, Adam was born in Lincoln Hospital and suffered no ill effects from his first secret appearance on stage.

It is believed that although the pantomime is based upon the life of a real man – Richard Whittington, one-time Lord Mayor of London, that the cat's origins are somewhat different. Whittington was a prosperous London merchant who owned coal barges – which in those days were known as 'cats'.

Mother brought in the New Year of 1962 with her usual bang by re-arranging the furniture in the sitting room and pushing the piano so hard that it fell on its back, crashed into the television and broke its legs. I managed to knock both mother and father off their feet by dropping my own clanger: Kenneth had asked me to marry him and I had accepted.

95.

32. *Dick Whittington at the Lincoln Repertory Theatre. In addition to the professional actors 'The Pippins' can be seen front L. and R.*
(see text)

I had been down to London with Kenneth for a few days, staying with my cousin Tricia, to help him with the auditions to select new actors for the spring season. It was in London that Kenneth had proposed.

The first people to whom we had broken the news were Freddie Jones and James Loughran who joined us for a celebratory drink in a pub around the corner from Dinely Studios where the auditions were held. It was a somewhat strained engagement party: Freddie overflowing with bonhomie and James, now embarked on what would be a hugely successful career as a conductor, having already managed to acquire a certain *gravitas*. I had my own worries. As I was only eighteen, Kenneth still had to ask my father's permission for my hand – assuming we wished to marry before my twenty-first birthday – which we did.

My parents were justifiably lukewarm about the proposal. I was still in my teens and Kenneth almost thirteen years my senior. He was also in a profession which might well ensure that I would never be bored but could never ensure that I would be secure. But love is stubborn, and my parents gave in to my wishes.

Kenneth had been director of productions at Lincoln Theatre for over five years and even before our engagement had decided it was time to move on. Our decision to marry gave him added impetus to further his career elsewhere.

Before he left Lincoln at the end of May, the theatre enjoyed a string of successful productions: Philip Madoc appeared in *Black Coffee*; Freddie Jones returned to play Uncle Arthur Broadbent in Waterhouse and Hall's marvellous northern comedy *Celebration*; and Brigit Forsyth played Jane in the delicious musical *Salad Days*.

Such an innocently romantic story of young love would soon become a period piece, for 'Love Me Do' by the Beatles was released and Beatlemania rushed in the new style sixties – peace, love, pot and the Pill. By the end of August Marilyn Monroe was dead at the age of 36 and as the cult of youth started to take over the media, her death also signalled the end of an era: that of the glossy and glamorous Hollywood films.

In October, Lincoln hosted its own film – a midnight matinee of *The Wild and the Willing* which had been shot almost entirely on location in the city. The Assize Court building was turned into a university for the film and many residents of Lincoln spent happy days as film extras in scenes shot around the Castle, Steep Hill, and the High Street.

Several feet were added to the top of the Observatory Tower at the Castle so that the character played by John Hurt (a former Lincoln School pupil), could plunge to his death when a university prank misfired. Catherine Woodville, who had been employed briefly at Lincoln Theatre some time earlier, now returned to Lincoln triumphantly as one of the stars of the film.

It was an understandable hit in Lincoln and was held over for an extra week; but generally cinema audiences were declining. In 1960 the Radion and Grand cinemas had closed – killed by television – the same year in which the wedding of Princess Margaret and Anthony Armstrong Jones was watched by an estimated 300 million television viewers worldwide.

Lincoln had started to 'modernise' itself by defacing charming old buildings or knocking them down and replacing them with new ones in a style best described as 'architectural brutalism'. A hideous blue cladding would be superimposed on the dignified facade of the Mawer & Collingham building in 1962. Wesley Chapel – 'Big Wesley' – on Clasketgate which had seated fifteen hundred people, and where my Aunt Maud had sung and we had applauded, was demolished in 1963 and replaced by a soulless, faceless office block.

Larder's Provisions and Drapery Shop on Nettleham village green had been taken over by the Co-operative Society in 1949 and that building too would be pulled down and replaced by one in such insensitively inappropriate style that it destroyed for ever the harmony of the village green and its encircling houses. The architect and whoever had given permission for its erection should have been banished to the darkness of Legoland.

Soon a new development of modern houses and bungalows (the first of many) would be built in and around Nettleham, transforming the close-knit rural community of my childhood into an ever-extending dormitory for Lincoln; its narrow streets choked with parked cars; its High Street transformed into a dangerous race track. Instead of children wandering and exploring as they pleased – an intrinsic part of the visible, daily life of the village – the majority of them would be driven to and from school in their mothers' cars, like so many legless parcels.

The slopes running down to the vicarage where, muffled in scarves and mittens, we'd eagerly dragged our sledges at the first sign of snow, would vanish under bricks and mortar. The little copse of trees where we'd received our first experimental and innocent kisses would now be overlooked by voyeuristic picture windows.

It is easy now, in middle age, to feel belatedly protective towards the place where I grew up; to resent what some call progress and I see only as change. Yet I think it fair to acknowledge that my generation is probably the last to have been fortunate enough to reach maturity in a country where society was coherent and unthreatening rather than fragmented and polarised as it seems to be today.

But like so many young people then, I'd become increasingly bored by the confines of my Lincolnshire childhood life and was keen to welcome any changes. Bonds of community and rigid moral conventions were slackening. I'd tugged at mine by working in the theatre and now, by marrying and moving away to start a new peripatetic life, I was stretching them further.

Having been protected by our family upbringing and disciplined education; encouraged by parents who wanted us to enjoy the freedom and opportunities which they had been denied because of the war, we were arrogantly secure and convinced the best was yet to come.

As the family-oriented fifties, filled with innocent promise, yielded to the swinging sixties – the years of *Lady Chatterley's Lover*, the Beatles, and the Pill – it was my generation that ensured society would never be the same again.

Crossing over:
The new bridge over the Nettleham beck.

Where the brook and river meet,
Womanhood and childhood fleet!

Deep and still, that gliding stream
Beautiful to thee must seem,
As the river of a dream.

100.

33. *Wedding Day — 2nd June 1963*

'— May glides onward into June.'